New Directions for
Teaching and Learning

Marilla D. Svinicki
EDITOR-IN-CHIEF

R. Eugene Rice
CONSULTING EDITOR

Identity, Learning, and the Liberal Arts

Ned Scott Laff
EDITOR

Number 103 • Fall 2005
Jossey-Bass
San Francisco

IDENTITY, LEARNING, AND THE LIBERAL ARTS
Ned Scott Laff (ed.)
New Directions for Teaching and Learning, no. 103
Marilla D. Svinicki, Editor-in-Chief
R. Eugene Rice, Consulting Editor

Microfilm copies of issues and articles are available in 16mm and 35mm, as well as microfiche in 105mm, through University Microfilms Inc., 300 North Zeeb Road, Ann Arbor, Michigan 48106-1346.

NEW DIRECTIONS FOR TEACHING AND LEARNING (ISSN 0271-0633, electronic ISSN 1536-0768) is part of The Jossey-Bass Higher and Adult Education Series and is published quarterly by Wiley Subscription Services, Inc., A Wiley Company, at Jossey-Bass, 989 Market Street, San Francisco, California 94103-1741. Periodicals postage paid at San Francisco, California, and at additional mailing offices. POSTMASTER: Send address changes to New Directions for Teaching and Learning, Jossey-Bass, 989 Market Street, San Francisco, California 94103-1741.

New Directions for Teaching and Learning is indexed in College Student Personnel Abstracts, Contents Pages in Education, and Current Index to Journals in Education (ERIC).

SUBSCRIPTIONS cost $80 for individuals and $170 for institutions, agencies, and libraries. Prices subject to change. See order form at end of book.

EDITORIAL CORRESPONDENCE should be sent to the editor-in-chief, Marilla D. Svinicki, Department of Educational Psychology, University of Texas at Austin, One University Station, D5800, Austin, TX 78712.

www.josseybass.com

Contents

FROM THE SERIES EDITOR

About This Publication. Since 1980, *New Directions for Teaching and Learning* (NDTL) has brought a unique blend of theory, research, and practice to leaders in postsecondary education. *NDTL* sourcebooks strive not only for solid substance but also for timeliness, compactness, and accessibility.

The series has four goals: to inform readers about current and future directions in teaching and learning in postsecondary education, to illuminate the context that shapes these new directions, to illustrate these new directions through examples from real settings, and to propose ways in which these new directions can be incorporated into still other settings.

This publication reflects the view that teaching deserves respect as a high form of scholarship. We believe that significant scholarship is conducted not only by researchers who report results of empirical investigations but also by practitioners who share disciplined reflections about teaching. Contributors to *NDTL* approach questions of teaching and learning as seriously as they approach substantive questions in their own disciplines, and they deal not only with pedagogical issues but also with the intellectual and social context in which these issues arise. Authors deal on the one hand with theory and research and on the other with practice, and they translate from research and theory to practice and back again.

About This Volume. Many claims are made for the value of liberal studies in developing more than just the academic skills of our students. This volume of *New Directions for Teaching and Learning* argues that we must foster a conversation between those in liberal studies and those who work with student development theory. This conversation reveals that the skills of academic inquiry inherent in liberal learning are the skills of personal development inherent in student development theory. This issue tackles the ideas of liberal learning and outlines a pedagogical direction to realize them.

Marilla D. Svinicki
Editor-in-Chief

MARILLA D. SVINICKI is associate professor of educational psychology at the University of Texas at Austin.

EDITOR'S NOTES

On my campus, as on many others, we have been involved in a core renewal. Our discussions reflect the debates on liberal learning. We hope our efforts will end in a learning experience that affects our students intellectually, ethically, and personally. We hope we can promote their sense of social justice and engaged citizenship. In line with national agendas, such as that of the Association of American Colleges and Universities (AAC&U), we hope our core learning provides our students with a transformative liberal learning experience.

What always hits me when I ask students—on my campus or the ones I visit—if they understand core learning is that it never seems to take root in their thinking that core learning plays a critical role in helping them think with, think about, and think through issues that speak directly to them. Despite our best intentions, core learning is not speaking to students' lives; it is not transformative. For that, something else is needed.

This volume is a step to finding that "something else." It developed from my experience with the students in my classes, working in the Unit One Living-Learning Center at the University of Illinois at Urbana-Champaign, developing advising programs, developing first-year experience courses, and collaborating with those versed in student development theory. Each contributor also comes with experience in bridging the gap between their academic commitments and the role development theory can play in helping them to clarify how they design student learning encounters.

Our collective aim is to explore how we can incorporate what we call a developmental underpinning into our thinking about liberal learning and our learning strategies in core courses and common areas of students' experience on campus. This is intentional.

Chapter One argues that liberal learning can be a transformative experience in students' lives if we develop a conversation between those in liberal studies and those in student development theory. This conversation suggests that the skills of academic inquiry inherent to liberal learning are the skills also inherent to students' ethical, moral, and character development.

Chapter Two argues that if we intentionally design assignments around "ill-structured" problems, we challenge students to become initiated into the practice of higher-order thinking and the ability to develop personal commitments through inquiring, reflecting, and arguing. This process fosters intellectual and ethical development.

Chapter Three illustrates that by presenting ill-structured historical issues in debate formats we can foster a sense of civic responsibility and a sense of self. This format challenges students to rethink their understanding of issues and to reflect on how their rethinking forces them to rethink how they see themselves with the communities in which they live.

Chapter Four argues that science courses can have a broader effect on liberal studies students if we can design assignments so that students have a clear understanding of the nature of scientific inquiry. Students will not only learn science better, but they will also be able to consider the hidden impact that their understanding of science has on understanding themselves and their relationship to their world.

Chapter Five argues that service learning courses can affect cognitive, affective, and moral transformation, depending on how we incorporate the process of reflection into them. It traces one variation of the reflective process, the concept of liberation, arguing that the process of reflection enables students to take on learning itself as a liberating practice.

Chapter Six examines liberal learning in a residential living-learning center. By bringing together those in liberal studies with those in student development, it illustrates how living-learning centers provide a variety of avenues for students to explore new or controversial ideas in an environment designed to promote intellectual and personal development.

The challenge my colleagues and I have taken on in this volume is an attempt to outline a pragmatic approach to liberal learning that can ground our claims that liberal learning can be personally transformative. This volume is offered to those who, like us, believe in the role liberal learning can play in preparing our students to live within the complexities of global concerns.

Ned Scott Laff
Editor

NED SCOTT LAFF is coordinator for special academic projects and coordinator for core advising in the Office of the Vice President for Academic Affairs at Loyola University Chicago.

1

This chapter argues that liberal learning can be transformative and foster students' intellectual and ethical development only if we consider its development underpinnings and pedagogic strategies that illustrate that the skills of academic inquiry are the skills of personal development.

Setting the Stage for Identity, Learning, and the Liberal Arts

Ned Scott Laff

We debate continually about liberal education and the nature of liberal learning. We argue over the nature of the curriculum: Should it be grounded in the "canon?" Should it be inclusive? Should it be some mixture of both? Or should we change our focus altogether, not concentrating on specific courses but on learning outcomes that would characterize a liberally educated person? But then, we debate what learning outcomes would characterize a liberally educated person: Should outcomes focus on how students examine multiple interpretive possibilities? Or on how students understand how our sense of human values and justice are influenced by culture, historical events, and social forces? Or on how students acquire a technical and critical vocabulary to assess aesthetic influences? Or how students identify the critical questions of truth, morality, or social justice and are able to examine them from a philosophic or theological perspective? This line of inquiry leads to yet more questions: Which are the critical questions students should engage? Which narrative gives us our sense of culture and social forces? Which vocabulary should we choose? All that we seem to agree on is that no one curricular outline or proposal of liberal education can fit the contours of the diverse educational landscapes that colleges and universities present.

We also debate about the claims we make for liberal education. We claim that if our students engage liberal studies they will be challenged to engage issues of social justice, race and gender, and civic responsibilities. We claim that through their courses in liberal studies students will cultivate humanistic values, understand themselves better within the diversity of the global community, and develop a more empathetic consideration of their relationships with others. Fundamentally, we claim that through liberal studies students will learn to think about their lives in light of the texts we teach. And we claim that in doing so, liberal studies will inform our students' ethical, moral, and intellectual development, inspire a penchant for civic engagement, and instill in our students the habits of lifelong learning. Or so we hope.

While we have maintained a faith in the transformative nature of the liberal arts, that faith is challenged when we cannot say for certain that we are sure there is a relationship between the relevance we perceive in what we teach and the lives our students lead. Our intuitive sense based on anecdotal information leads us to argue that liberal education in fact does meet these claims, does in fact affect our students' cognitive and affective development, in large part because we reflect on how our own experiences with liberal education have affected our own lives. But we must be careful about our intuition. It can lead us to a false consensus. What may be the case for us simply may not be the case for our students. We may be right to be suspect of the claims we make about liberal studies. Consider two recent arguments debating the role of liberal studies: Martha Nussbaum's *Cultivating Humanity* (1997) and Jerry Graff's *Clueless in Academe* (2003), discussed below.

A Classical Defense of the "New" Liberal Studies

In *Cultivating Humanity* (1997), Nussbaum argues that the postmodern liberal-studies landscape is rooted in the classical Socratic enterprise. She maintains that it is from the Stoics and their applications of Socratic principles in designing educational institutions that "we derive our modern conception of liberal education" (p. 28). Nussbaum claims that our belief that liberal education challenges "the mind to take charge of its own thought" is Socratic in origin (p. 28). She identifies four claims about the Socratic basis of liberal education that characterize our views: it should be a part of every individual's self-realization; it should be suited to students' circumstances and context; it should be pluralistic, concerned with a variety of norms and traditions; and it should ensure that books do not become authorities but are themselves both examples of what "excellent thinking is like" and subject to critical inquiry (pp. 30–34).

With this as her contextual background, Nussbaum argues forcefully that the postmodern landscape of liberal studies is simply the latest iteration of the Socratic enterprise. Challenging critics such as Allan Bloom, Nussbaum claims that critical scrutiny of our cultural traditions and literary canon does not lead to cultural relativism, but rather leads to what can be defended rationally. For Nussbaum, the key to the postmodern liberal studies curriculum rests in the Socratic ideal of "living the examined life." Global studies, she asserts, finds its roots in Diogenes's self-description as a "citizen of the world" and "his image of the *kosmospolites,* or world citizen"

(p. 52). Cultural and literary studies find their roots in Marcus Aurelius's insistence that we develop in ourselves "a capacity for sympathetic imagination that will enable us to comprehend the motives and choices of people different from ourselves" (p. 85). Gender studies, based in Foucault's claim of sexuality as a social construct, is engaged, according to Nussbaum, in studying "the history and variety of human sexuality" (p. 225) and is linked to Socrates and his goal of living the examined life. Thus, the postmodern landscape is simply the next culturally progressive step in a tradition of liberal learning laid down from Socrates to Plato and Aristotle and actualized by Seneca and the Stoics.

As students take courses in what Nussbaum coins the "'New' Liberal Education," they will become inclined to "question, probe, and inquire" (p. 147). As important, students will be given a general preparation for citizenry locally, nationally, and globally. This, for Nussbaum, is a critical outcome. The New Liberal Education—at once Socratic and postmodern—cultivates our humanity by encouraging our students to understand their traditions and history, respect and appreciate the traditions and histories of others, and learn to move from the differences to a more pluralistic and mutual understanding. This lays the groundwork for what Nussbaum calls a "democratic culture that is truly deliberative and reflective, rather than simply a collision of unexamined preferences" (p. 294). Students will become characterized as liberal learners, she asserts, because from their course work they will take on the habits of critical self-examination; they will be liberated from habits of thinking and blindly accepting customs, traditions, and ideas without critically examining them; and they will empathize with others. By infusing the Socratic enterprise into the postmodern liberal-education landscape, Nussbaum believes, we establish a norm for our students' liberal learning and their citizenship.

Liberal Studies as Argument

Jerry Graff takes a different approach to the role liberal studies can play in students' lives in *Clueless in Academe* (2003). As Graff sees it, becoming liberally educated "has more to do with thinking and talking about subjects or texts in analytic ways than the subjects or text you study" (p. 222). Liberal learning is not grounded in any particular set of books or any particular curriculum. It can come from how we talk about our favorite sports team, the movies we like, or popular magazines and novels we read. Graff is convinced that liberal learning is rooted more in how much we are absorbed by what we read and that that absorption is more important than what we read. Perhaps most important is Graff's contention that liberal learning is evidenced by how we are able to talk about our absorptions. Liberal learning, then, is about how we are introduced to, engage with, and integrate into our lives what Graff calls the "culture of argument" (p. 23). It is this culture that characterizes what we in the academy do and what liberal learning is. For

Graff, argumentation is central to the academic enterprise and the liberal learning endeavor.

As Graff defines it, the culture of argument is about the "productive disagreements" that characterize how we work (p. 83). Graff contends that as we engage in conversation with other thinkers about ideas, theories, and interpretive analyses, we are forced to explicate our own thinking and assumptions and to look at subtexts and underlying meanings. Leaning on Robert Scholes (1985), Graff claims that through argumentative conversation of views and counterviews we learn "textual power," that is, how to move from simple perceptions about plots, events, and things (for example, that the film *Saving Private Ryan* is about soldiers in the throes of war) to reflective thematic observations (*Saving Private Ryan* provides a backdrop to explore human frailties, our selfishness, and doubt in moments of choice when we are asked to make personal sacrifices for comrades) (Graff, 2003, p. 181). Because these conversations are both comparative and synthetic, we generate from them new ideas, interpretive strategies, and theories. But liberal learning involves not simply how we read texts in class, but also how we read the underlying "cultural texts." We can turn to any subject around us (for example, Fox News, charity bracelets, or corporate logos) to see that textual power is also about how we perceive themes and values that are implied rather than stated in these cultural texts. But as important, says Graff, textual power is also about how we think about our relationship to these cultural texts. This, for Graff, is the liberal learning experience.

What makes Graff's discussion interesting is his claim that students are already unknowing neophytes in the culture of argument. As Graff is keen to point out, when students argue about the merits of their favorite team, hip-hop artists, or whether *Harry Potter* is better than *Lord of the Rings*, "they make claims, counterclaims, and value judgments" (p. 155). They use "rival texts, rival interpretations, and evaluations of texts and rival theories" on why they believe what they do (p. 220). What they often miss, according to Graff, is that their "street conversations" are the makings of the conversations that characterize the intellectual parlor room of academia (p. 158). They miss this because we keep the centrality of argument hidden from them. Graff argues we should pedagogically model how we converse with the critical controversies that make up the conversations in our disciplines, how we judge them, evaluate them, use them as interpretive tools, and synthesize our own positions using them. In doing so, we would introduce students to the vocabularies and the interpretive, evaluative, and rhetorical strategies that characterize the academic enterprise.

At the same time we would sharpen their personal critical lenses, their insights, and their abilities to express themselves cogently. These are the skills of textual power. By engaging students in learning how to use these skills, we open them to a more enhanced learning experience that ranges from the classroom to the workplace, from conversations with their friends to the exercise of democratic citizenship (p. 86). Through this, Graff contends, students discover their hidden intellectualism and the grounding for their liberal learning.

Interpreting Our Consensus of Belief

As should be apparent, I choose Nussbaum and Graff deliberately because each represents a different facet of the debate: Nussbaum arguing about the curriculum that makes up liberal studies and the claims we make for it, and Graff arguing about how we sharpen the claims we make about the skills from liberal studies that our students acquire. Both make claims about the transformative nature of liberal studies, and both ring similar to other debates we have heard before. Like others, both genuinely believe that if they can conjure their configuration by the right kind of incantation it will capture the force and purpose of liberal education and in so doing the minds, hearts, and dispositions of our students. But like others, except for their anecdotal arguments, which are quite appealing, they leave us suspicious. Like others, they are victims of the same flaw—this worked for us. If we can just lay out the steps to follow, our students, following those steps, will take on the habits of the heart that characterize the outcomes of liberal learning.

But our students are not us, and this is a rather critical point. The Association of American Colleges and Universities (AAC&U) confirms this insight. Carole Geary Schneider (2004), in reporting on focus groups AAC&U commissioned of college-bound high school seniors and college juniors and seniors conducted by Peter D. Hart Research Associates, notes an intriguing similarity. Students regard as important learning outcomes from liberal learning that stress one's ability to succeed on one's own, time-management, strong work habits, self-discipline, and teamwork. Their least-valued outcomes are values, principles, and ethics; tolerance and respect for different cultural backgrounds; expanded cultural and global awareness and sensitivity; and civic responsibility. Schneider points out that, despite our best intentions, we are not succeeding in helping our students become liberally educated.

Our problem in trying to develop an intentional approach to liberal learning may rest in our debates about the curriculum, the canon, and what we characterize as liberal learning. From Boyer to Bloom, from Hirsch to Bennett, we find ourselves transfixed looking for curricular models and identifying the learning outcomes associated with those models that will help us devise the liberal education experience we consider appropriate. We feel that if somehow we can prescribe whatever it is one has to know, then we can we guide students' learning so that they act as members of the liberally educated community. This puts us at risk of falling into a formalism that may very well work against us. To appreciate this situation we need only take a hint from Clifford Geertz's work, *The Interpretation of Cultures* (1973).

In critiquing ethnography, Geertz argued that a fault lay in the belief that an ethnographer could derive laws that would explain the behavior of people within a culture. As Geertz pointed out, the belief that we could derive the laws of a culture would lead us to believe as well that we could write out "systematical rules . . . which, if followed, would make it possible . . . to operate, to pass . . . for a native" (p. 11). But as Geertz pointed out, the questions then arise as to which analysis reflects what a people really think and whether any analyses may only be clever, logical imitations that fail to grasp the "imaginative universe" within which the acts and behaviors of a people take on "semiotic significance" (p. 11). Instead, Geertz argued, ethnographers should try to interpret and understand how a people structure meaning in order to grasp their cultural semantics.

There is a rough parallel here to our debates about liberal education. We seem to believe that if we can outline systematic curricular rules, these rules should make it possible, if followed, for anyone to pass as a member of the educational community. But this raises the question of whether any particular proposal reflects the educational enterprise. It also raises the question of whether students following these rules engage in learning experiences that affect their intellectual and personal growth or merely simulate and parody what our curricula call for. As Schneider's AAC&U study seems to indicate, it may unfortunately be the latter.

From Debate to Conversation

Lest it appear that I am simply a skeptic of liberal education, I mention here that I, too, have faith that liberal learning can be transformative. But that faith is challenged when we cannot say for certain that there is a relationship between what we perceive in what we teach and the lives our students lead. Debate about the nature of liberal studies curriculum may not be what we need.

Let us suppose for a moment that we can intentionally devise a liberal education experience that seduces our students into a dialogue with important questions of common concern (Bloom, 1987); that leads them to live responsible lives; challenges them to take ethical responsibility for their ideas and actions and to explore the relationship among their learning, their citizenship, and service; and that helps students realize the importance of understanding that we live within historical, cultural, global, and pluralistic contexts. Let us also agree with the AAC&U's Statement on Liberal Learning (1998) that such learning is not confined to particular fields of study. What matters is that liberal learning has "substantial content, rigorous methodology, and an active engagement with the societal, ethical, and practical implications of our learning" (n.p.).

The claims we make for liberal learning are claims about how it transforms our personal lives and our personal development. What we have found compelling in liberal learning is that it has helped us fundamentally to think about our identity, our personal growth, and our lives. We have found that liberal learning lets us deal with the unending negotiation and renegotiation of the meaning of experiences to ourselves.

What makes this argument intriguing is that Carol Gilligan (1981), a development theorist, has noted that personal development is similarly rooted in "a continuing interplay of thought and experience" (p. 156). In other words, Gilligan is suggesting that our reflections on our engagement with liberal learning and our reflections on our personal development may have structurally functional similarities. Development revolves around how we learn to think; how we learn to ask questions; and how we come up with solutions, whether it be to the neatly formulated problems of the classroom or the logically messy problems of real life. This is no less true for our students. And this is where we may be compelled to turn to find a way to ground our anecdotal claims about liberal learning.

Those in liberal studies and student development theorists rarely talk with each other. However, such a conversation would illustrate a remarkable commonality that both share. Consider William Perry* (1970), one of the seminal thinkers in student development theory. As Perry has argued, how students meet the challenges they encounter in their academic work, co-curricular activities, and social life are tied to the ways they perceive their world, understand it, and generate values. The confrontation with the pluralism of values becomes inescapable and one of the purposes of the college experience is to present students with the questions we have continually raised for ourselves and which we have spent our history, according to Perry, "trying to resolve, rephrase, and learn to live with" (p. 33). For Perry, college affords students the opportunity to learn to question their own lines of reasoning to the challenges each faces in their own particular ways, and to test their assumptions and their reasoning against the reasoning of others. This, for Perry, is the characteristic of a liberally educated individual—a personal commitment to resist leading an unexamined life.

Perry suggests that the skills of academic inquiry and personal development overlap and reveal a common pattern: "Students' restructuring in their view of the world is characteristic of the evolution of scientific theory (Kuhn, 1970). Strangely enough, we have found no explicit description of this kind of transformation as a phenomenon in human personal development. As a strategy of growth it would deserve a prominent place, not only in a theory of cognitive development but also in consideration of emotional maturation and the formation of identity" (p. 110).

To appreciate what Perry is claiming, we need only compare the basic concepts from developmental theory—those of Perry himself—and T.S. Kuhn's thoughts in *The Structure of Scientific Revolutions* (1970), a work that has proved seminal across the liberal arts disciplines. We would find the structural similarities to be striking. In fact, we would discover, as Perry hinted, that the processes are the same.

The Perry-Kuhn Conversation

Perry's concern is to describe and understand the "evolution in students' interpretation of their lives" that consists of their progression through "certain forms [or structures] in which the students construe their experience" (Perry, 1970, p. 1). By "forms" or "structures," Perry means the relatively stable relations of "assumptions and expectations a person holds at any given time" by which she or he construes experience (p. 42). Development theorists are used to discussing the characteristic attribute of their forms, such as dualism, relativism, and so on. But it is important for us to also consider that these forms function as personal theories. This specificity becomes more explicit with the help of Kuhn.

Perry's forms satisfy the same criteria Kuhn (1970) uses to describe paradigms. A paradigm is an accepted pattern of methodological beliefs that affect how we see, interpret, and evaluate experience and how we articulate and solve problems. Paradigms help us make sense of experience because they appear to reveal the nature of things; they allow us to predict in an attempt to bring our assumptions and expectations closer to the nature of things; and they let us further articulate our understanding by helping us explore and interpret new experience.

Kuhn is quick to point out, however, that paradigms are open-ended, leaving problems to be solved and many facts and events we confront through the paradigm unexplained. Normally, work through the paradigm is cumulative, extending the scope and precision of our understanding by assimilating the solutions, problems, and new data into the parameters of the paradigm and, at the same time, adjusting the paradigm to account for things that do not quite fit. Research under the paradigm is a "particularly effective way of inducing paradigm change" (Kuhn, 1970, p. 52). Paradigm-based research is interactive and repeatedly brings up new and unsuspected phenomena—anomalies—that cannot be assimilated into the paradigm. Anomalies appear only against the background provided by the paradigm's context, which provides us a sense that "nature has somehow violated the paradigm-induced expectations that govern normal science" (pp. 52–53). The perception of anomalies leads to a "crisis," a failure of the normal problem-solving activities of the paradigm.

These points of crisis are critical because they open up the difficulties in the paradigm-nature fit. Kuhn explains that crises challenge previously held standard beliefs and procedures along with stereotypes; they call into question the paradigm's explicit and fundamental generalizations. Faced with a breakdown, normal science seeks a transition to a new paradigm, a reconstruction that changes some of the field's generalizations, methods, and applications by discarding some previously standard practices and replacing them with others. These revolutionary paradigm shifts, in turn, affect changes in worldview. Through the new paradigm we see old terms, concepts, and events in different relationship to one another. The shift opens up a wider range of phenomena, providing greater precision for explanation and providing better ways of perceiving and acting in the world.

The course of normal science is an interpretive enterprise articulated through paradigms. And normal science leads to acceptance of paradigms, the recognition of anomalies, and to crises. The successive transition from one paradigm to another, as Kuhn argues, is the normal developmental pattern. And transition is driven by scientific method.

Kuhn's Structure of Scientific Revolutions. The following is my outline of Kuhn's scheme.

Paradigm: An accepted pattern of theoretical and methodological beliefs that affect how we see, interpret, and evaluate; how we make sense of things and solve problems; and how we explore and interpret new experiences.

Open-Endedness: Paradigms extend the scope of our understanding, but they also bring up problems and facts that the paradigm can neither solve nor explain.

Anomalies: New and unsuspected phenomena are anomalies. They appear only against the background of the paradigm, which provided the context that "nature" has somehow violated the paradigm-induced expectations.

Crisis: When significant anomalies develop they point out the failure of the normal problem-solving activities of the paradigm, challenging the beliefs and generalizations of the paradigm.

Restructuring or New Paradigm Development: Faced with a breakdown, "science" seeks a transition to a new paradigm, a restructuring that changes some of the generalizations, methods, and applications. This "paradigm shift" affects changes in worldview, lets us see old terms, concepts, things, and events in different relationships to each other, and re-educates our ways of perceiving and acting in the world.

Note: This is an ongoing activity.

We can infer from Kuhn that Perry's "forms of expectancies" (p. 42) are personal paradigms and that Perry is also trying to provide a sense of the dynamics of personal paradigm shift, left largely inferential behind the static descriptions of developmental positions. Meaning emerges as we interact through our personal paradigms with the diversity of real-world experiences. Our forms of expectancies extend through our thoughts, feelings, actions, and interactions—they are our personal methodologies. They help us discover and expand our world by letting us meet the challenges of diversity with a minimum of incongruity. They provide us with a coherent view of the world as long as we can assimilate the consequences of our interactions by means of selection, simplification, and sometimes slanted interpretation.

Our forms (personal paradigms) are also open-ended because we find they do not always work. They cause us to misinterpret and to make mistakes.

These mistakes raise incongruities and uncertainties between the personal paradigm-experience fit, which challenge us to come to grips with the limits of our personal paradigms. In turn, we are challenged to consider whether the assumptions underlying our personal paradigm-induced expectations give us a good working sense of how things are.

These incongruities are anomalies, and they jolt our picture of the world. Their build-up leads to crisis and impels us to challenge, reorganize, and sometimes dissolve established beliefs. Crisis leads us to challenge stereotypic thinking and unexamined commitments. Crisis demands new decisions and requires reconstruction of the old paradigmatic structure to resolve the crises and to help us reinterpret our interactions. The transitional process by which we create new forms of expectancy leads to a revolutionary shift in our personal paradigms and better ways of perceiving and acting in the world.

Perry's "Forms" of Intellectual and Ethical Development. Here is my outline of Perry's concept of "forms."

Forms of Expectancies: These are relatively stable assumptions and expectations a person holds at any given time by which she or he construes and makes sense of experiences, providing a coherent view of the world.

Open-Endedness: Interaction, the diversity of real-world experience, raises problems with the fit between a "form of expectancy" and experience.

Mistakes and Misinterpretations: Mistakes arise because a form does not account for new, different, or unexpected experiences, challenging the reliability of the form.

Crisis: When mistakes reach a certain level we are challenged to consider that our assumptions and the expectancies that underlie our forms may not be giving us a good working sense of how things are, jolting our picture of the world and raising questions about whether our form is adequate.

Reorganization and Reconstruction: Crisis leads us to reconstruct our form to take into consideration the old form and accommodate for the mistakes. This changes our worldview, allowing us to reinterpret our interactions, resolve the problem with the form-experience fit, and provide a better way of perceiving and acting in the world.

Note: This is an on-going process.

The Skills of Liberal Learning as the Skills of Personal Development

Granted, I have abbreviated much. But enough is outlined to suggest that Kuhn and Perry are talking about the same things—the pattern of revolutionary restructuring in the ways we view and interact in the world. For Kuhn, the emphasis is on the paradigms underlying fields of study;

for Perry, the emphasis is on students, the evolution of their personal paradigms, and how they create personal meaning.

Academic Inquiry as Personal Development. The following schematic comparison illustrates the Perry-Kuhn convergence.

Academic Inquiry:	Personal Development:
Theory Building (Kuhn)	*Student Development Theory (Perry)*
Paradigm	*Form of Expectancy*
Open-Endedness	*Open-Endedness*
Anomalies	*Mistakes*
Crisis	*Crisis*
Restructure or Create New Paradigm	*Reorganization or Create New Form*
Growth in Knowledge	*Personal Growth*

The same process of transition seems to underlie both. As Perry notes, "Students conceptualize more frequently in periods of . . . confrontation with incongruity, and when a new higher order concept has proved itself generally viable, it tends to embed itself into the new *perception* of 'how things are' until dislodged by some fresh incongruity" (p. 93).

Developmental transitions may very well be based in what we might readily describe as the personal research activities from which all paradigms are created. The transitional process underlying developmental theory is common to liberal learning. These skills of personal research—raising questions, seeking alternative views, discovering, interpreting, hypothesizing, and evaluating—are productive critical thinking skills which, perhaps not so surprisingly, are the skills we talk of in liberal learning. This congruence provides us with a ground to claim that the skills of academic inquiry are the skills of personal development.

Part of our solution, then, in helping students feel the immediacy of the relationship between their liberal education experiences and their lives is helping them experience in real ways that the problems they are assigned and work through in their classes are like other problems they face daily. This is no less than helping students demonstrate for themselves how to perceive the analogy between how we think in class and how "we understand experience metaphorically when we use the gestalt from one domain of experience to give us insight into another domain" (Lakoff and Johnson, 1980, p. 230). The Perry-Kuhn conversation contextualizes our claims that liberal education is transformative and provides a ground for general problem solving. The conversation gives us grounds to argue that liberal education is no less than helping students master the critical skills for their own personal paradigmatic shifts and development.

The Imaginative Experiment

The context of the Perry-Kuhn conversation, then, provides us insight into how liberal studies can catalyze our students' evolution in the way they interpret their world and themselves within it. The underlying common thread in this conversation is how we make sense of our interaction with the incongruities of experience. For Kuhn it is our search for understanding phenomena and events; for Perry it is in understanding ourselves as we interact within the world we live in. What drives both is how we use the parameters of liberal learning—both content and skills—to make sense of our contextual encounters.

On one level, the Perry-Kuhn context speaks to the claims made by Jerry Graff that I have outlined above. The distinction between the skills of academic inquiry and the skills we use every day to make sense of things may not be great, if different at all. Consider, for example, basic rhetorical modes such as comparison and contrast, description, evaluation, or definition. Rhetorical modes are not simply compositional strategies. We use these rhetorical strategies in everyday conversation, and we also use them to make sense of things—our likes and dislikes, what we value, and how we explain the ideas and things that are important to us and shape who we are. They are part and parcel of our educational and personal critical thinking skills. What liberal learning affords is an opportunity to pull out these tacit skills and focus on how we understand them and how we use them. In a very real sense, through liberal learning, as Graff argues, when we "let students in on the secret that intellectual writing and discussions are extensions of their normal conversational practices" we can begin to help students put the skills of liberal learning into conversation with their lives (Graff, 2003, p. 58). The same is true for other critical thinking skills embedded across liberal education disciplines.

On another level, Perry talks about nothing less than students assuming responsibility to examine their "personal commitments in a relative world" (p. 34). As Perry puts it, what is required for students, and us, to assume this responsibility is a "capacity for detachment" (p. 35). We must be able to stand back from our lives, have a good look at ourselves as we interact, critically examine our interactions, and then go back into our lives with a new sense of our own personal responsibilities to make meaningful sense these interactions. Perry argues that this act of standing back "is forced" in liberal education "by the impact of pluralism of values and points of view" (p. 35). This argument rings to the claims made by Martha Nussbaum. Perry explicates the developmental underpinnings that can justify Nussbaum's argument that the Socratic enterprise grounds the new liberal education. Like Perry, Nussbaum argues that we do not "cultivate our own humanity" without critically examining our own traditions within a pluralistic context" (Nussbaum, 1997, p. 295). Making the Socratic argument of the new liberal education part of our students' lives, as Nussbaum sees it, challenges both those who argue against simply acculturating our students into the conventions and traditions of Western culture and those who argue about the threat that our students will become uncritical moral relativists. Students will be challenged to rethink their own views and take ownership of their choices, beliefs, and values.

The Perry-Kuhn conversation gives warrant to our claims that the process and content of liberal studies can challenge our students' understanding of the world they believe they know, charge students' intellectual and narrative imaginations, and provide a virtual context for them to interact with experiences they normally may never have within a developmental context. It gives us warrant to believe that liberal education can be transformative because our students encounter incongruities of experience that liberal studies afford, creating "mistakes," "anomalies," and "crises" that catalyze the nature of liberal learning and personal development. In other words, these skills of academic inquiry as skills of personal development lay bare that intellectual and personal development are part and parcel of the same meaning-making process; they sit on the same continuum. What is intriguing is that we do recognize in this that the fundamentals of academic inquiry, whether we call it "scientific method" or simply "scholarly research," work across the continuum. Louise Rosenblatt (1995) has argued this point in *Literature as Exploration*. Liberal education, characterized by the Kuhn-Perry conversation, sets the ground for what Rosenblatt has called the "imaginative experimentation" (p. 190) that can drive students' developmental encounters.

Rosenblatt believes that the "vicarious experiences" afforded by literature in fact lead to an "enlargement" of students' overall life experiences (p. 190). As Rosenblatt argues, "the ability to picture oneself in a variety of situations and to envisage alternative modes of behavior and their consequences" are the things that characterize the wisdom gained from literary studies (p. 190). For Rosenblatt, the reader's life situations are not unique or significantly different from those in the stories and poetry they read, and so their life experiences provide at least minimal parallels to understanding and empathizing with the others they meet through their reading—adolescents struggling to achieve a new sense of themselves; couples living through the fuzzy and oftentimes confusing dynamics of relationships; men and women trying to find meaning, recognition, and belief in an indifferent world; the ongoing struggle with sexual identity, racial equality and dignity, and gender roles. These and much more provide a means for readers to vicariously experience another's life, another's emotions, and try these out against the context of their own life. Rosenblatt argues that these vicarious experiences let students experience problems apart from themselves and help them "to think and feel more clearly about them" (p. 191). This is no less than Perry's "capacity for detachment" (p. 35).

Liberal Learning and the Narrative Imagination

Rosenblatt takes this thinking a few steps further. By charging students' narrative imaginations, we provide them the opportunity to "go through a process of imaginative trial and error, trying out different modes of behavior and working our their probable effects" (p. 190). For Rosenblatt, this is imaginative experimenting: "We can live different types of lives; we can anticipate future periods in our own life; we can participate in different social settings; we can try out solutions to personal problems. We are able to apprehend the practical and emotional results, the reactions of others, the social praise or blame that may flow from such conduct" (p. 190).

Rosenblatt's point here is grounded in our common belief that we develop a better understanding of our world and ourselves within it by looking at and reflecting on the personal and social expressions and attitudes of others. Literature provides an imaginative experimental context in which students encounter open-endedness, mistakes, crisis, and rethinking within the plots they engage and the characters they encounter. And this, Rosenblatt argues, can lead to personal growth. The skills of literary study that provide students the tools to evaluate the works they read and their reading responses to them also provide students with the skills they need to reflect upon their "reading responses" to their own interactions within the communities they live in and the realities we construct socially.

Literary study is but one area within the liberal arts landscape for imaginative experimenting with the behaviors, social attitudes, concepts of standards and ideals, and social relationships reflective of the cultural heterogeneity in which we live. It does not take much of an analogic leap to see how we can extend Rosenblatt's idea of the imaginative experiment across liberal studies. Each discipline within the liberal arts, in its own way, puts in front of students problems and situations that, to play off Rosenblatt, provide an imaginative experimental encounter that holds the potential to challenge how students understand the meaning they create of their interactive experiences. By playing off Rosenblatt's cue, students can "experience" the needs and problems of different social groups; "experience" the workings of political and social actions and theories of those removed from their daily lives; or "try on" alternative philosophies, patterns of behavior, or spiritual beliefs. This imaginative experimenting brings together the different ways disciplines solve problems and reflect. This process holds promise to help students experience the personal values embedded when their personal paradigms are challenged through liberal learning. And this makes all the more sense within the context of the Perry-Kuhn conversation.

From Composite View to a Pedagogical Direction

We now have many of the pieces to sketch a composite of sorts from which we can pragmatically argue and ground our anecdotal sense that liberal learning can be transformative. We can now argue that the skills of academic inquiry that students learn and use that underlie liberal study are similar to, if not the same as, the skills they use for their personal intellectual and ethical development. The areas of study that make up liberal learning, we can argue metaphorically, provide and expand students' interactive encounters with the communities they live in locally, nationally, and globally. We can argue that how liberal learning helps students understand the ways we socially construct meaning is similar to, if not the same as, the ways students learn to understand how they construct their personal meanings and their personal paradigms. Finally, we can argue that students' interactive experiences with liberal studies, like their daily interactive experiences, lend themselves to open-endedness that can catalyze development by providing them the opportunity to exercise their contextual and critical thinking skills to understand their interactions with new contexts, examine how those new contexts can challenge their ways of understanding, and develop the skills to re-contextualize their personal paradigms. The Perry-Kuhn conversation reveals these striking congruencies.

It would seem, then, that if we want to claim that our students do realize liberal learning experiences in our programs, these attributes would be embedded within other learning outcomes we outline for our courses and other learning experiences on campus. This claim raises a number of critical points: Can we glean from this composite a pedagogical direction that we might explore that could help us incorporate these attributes as part and parcel of our students' liberal learning experiences? Could we ensure that this pedagogical direction would not compromise course content and coverage or other more standard learning outcomes we outline for our students? Would such a pedagogical direction mean that we would have to make significant changes in what we do in our classes or could such a pedagogical direction be easily incorporated into our existing classroom strategies and techniques? Finally, could we find a pedagogical direction that could fit equally well in classroom settings and co-curricular settings? Again, we can find the clues in the Perry-Kuhn conversation, and again, we will find the congruence in thinking about these points to be striking.

Perry, as I have mentioned, believes that the liberal learning experience, because it presents a "pluralism of values and points of view," is especially conducive to foster students' ethical and moral development and their abilities to make personal commitments in a relative world (p. 35). For Perry, the impact of liberal learning on students can be significant if it is "intentional on the part of individual professors" (p. 35). This impact comes from interacting with the diversity of the educational environment. It could come from a student's interacting through liberal learning that presents views that students have not engaged. It could come from the "clash" of different faculty in different courses who are sure that each teaches the "truth." But as Perry argues, the impact is most effective when it is deliberate: "When a teacher asks his students to read conflicting authorities and then asks them to assess the nature and meaning of the conflict, he is in a strong position to assist them to go beyond simple diversity into the disciplines of relativity of thought through which specific instances of diversity can be productively exploited. He can teach relation, the relativism, of one system of thought to another. In short, he can teach disciplined independence of mind" (p. 35).This is teaching controversy and conflict by intent, and for Perry, it marks the character of good teaching.

If this rings familiar to us, it should. Jerry Graff (1992) has argued a similar point but with a different emphasis. In *Beyond the Culture Wars,* Graff contended that we should make productive use of the conflicts in our fields. We should teach them. His point is that by doing so we would introduce students to the nature of our academic culture and to how we do our work and how we create our fields of study. Graff believes that in presenting our debates to students we help them realize that we construct knowledge. By demonstrating, for example, different critical perspectives and ideological positions on the same topic, book, or event, we can engage students in one of the more provocative questions that underlies our work— "How do we know?" Using the debates in our field, we can challenge students to look at how different positions make different claims and bring up different interpretations of the same material. They will be challenged by the conversations to examine how different positions make their case and we can use this process to help students develop their own interpretations by helping them understand that their thinking always takes place within the contrasting context of a dialogue. Like Perry, Graff argues for teaching conflict by intent, but his purpose is that doing so will introduce students to the nature of university learning.

Liberal Learning as Problem-Based

Teaching conflict by intent still leaves us with the question of how to teach conflict by design. Neither Perry nor Graff provides a scheme—they merely point us in the direction of one. The common elements for both are how we intentionally create open-endedness for students; how we make use of the continuing interplay between our thinking and our interacting with the logical fuzziness inherent in liberal learning and our daily encounters; and how we provide our students with the challenge of posing questions, thinking about solutions, and thinking about how their solutions stack up in conversation with others. We recognize these elements as part of the benchmarks of problem-based learning, and it is here that we may find a pedagogical direction. This should not surprise us.

Kurt Burch's outline of problem-based learning (2001) provides a good sense of why this approach lends itself to teaching conflict by design and fostering personal development. As Burch notes, because students interact with each other and with the course material, they engage in "a shared enterprise of learning-by-discovery" where they discover as much about themselves as they do about the topics they study (p. 194). Problem-based learning challenges students with responsibility to decide collaboratively how to solve the problems that are posed to them. It does so, according to Burch, because a well-devised problem "transports students from the classroom to tangible, real-world situations" (p. 194). One of the central principles, according to Burch, is that problems are open-ended. "Well-devised problems provide insufficient information for immediate solution" (p. 194). In other words, well-devised problems are ill-structured and logically fuzzy. These ill-structured problems challenge students to think about how what they know can be used to work through the problem, to think about what they do not understand about the problem and what they do not know, and to think about the assumptions they carry with them that can color the way they may read and misread the problem. Well-devised problems challenge students' paradigms of knowing and provide a two-fold experience: that of seeing that we are constantly rethinking how we know things and the actual experience of rethinking how we know. It is easy to imagine how a problem-based approach fits with the logical fuzziness inherent in liberal learning across the curriculum and in the diversity of students' encounters on campus.

There is a second important principle: students work in groups to discuss the problem. A problem-oriented approach is collaborative. It lends itself to how we want to devise learning groups within our classes, learning communities, first-year interest groups, and co-curricular engagements. It can lend itself to how we use Blackboard technology, or the like, to create problem-driven chat rooms and threaded discussions. Burch (2001) notes that part of the learning that takes place through a problem-based approach is that students must learn to coordinate their efforts, cooperate to reach a collective goal, and collaborate in presenting what they find (p. 195). In this, students mirror Graff's conversations. Through dialogue, students are challenged to look at how their interpretation of the problem differs from that of their peers, and they are challenged to look at how the assumptions that make up their personal paradigms influence their interpretation of the problem. In this way, they experience how our problem solving takes place within the context of a dialogue, leading to how we construct and reconstruct what we know. More interesting, through the collaborative conversations students experience what Perry defines as being liberally educated—learning how to think about their own thinking, to examine the ways they order and interpret information, and learning to examine assumptions and to compare these assumptions with the thinking of others (Perry, 1970, p. 39).

Problem-based learning provides the scheme to design student encounters with incongruity, open-endedness, mistakes, crisis, and rethinking, either in the classroom or in co-curricular activities. It provides a scheme to design the conversational encounters in which students will have to look at how they think in relation to others. Our task in teaching is to guide students in using the research and critical thinking skills of academic inquiry to think out the problems, think about the mistakes that inevitably arise from their encounter with the incongruities and logical fuzziness inherent in the problems, leading them to learn how to learn. As Burch is quick to point out, through "the process, students develop new social and cognitive skills, responsibilities, and understandings" (pp. 194–195). A problem-based learning approach is the last piece to synthesizing this composite.

Conclusion

Admittedly, I have paid short shrift to how we actually can use a problem-based learning approach in a classroom or other learning encounters that students engage in. I have left this to my colleagues who have contributed to this volume. Each speaks to a core area of students' liberal learning experiences and co-curricular experiences in service learning and residential living-learning centers. Each, in one iteration or another, leans on different aspects of the Perry-Kuhn conversation. And each illustrates that by simply recasting some of the questions we ask of our students and the context within which we ask those questions, we affect, sometimes significantly, the ways students interact with their educational environment and the immediacy of how their liberal learning speaks to their lives. What they demonstrate is the ease with which we can incorporate this composite into our day-to-day pedagogic strategies and any of our campus interactions with students. My intent here is to focus on outlining a conceptual underpinning for our claims that liberal learning can be an interactive, transformative experience for students.

If we believe that liberal learning can be transformative it is because there is reason lurking in our intuition that encourages us. What we find in the Perry-Kuhn conversation is a confluence of our anecdotal suspicions, our common sense, and our theoretical perspective. This synthesizing of what we already know and the grounding that comes from this conversation holds promise to help us, as Perry would have it, intentionally design open-ended encounters with learning. Perry has argued that as we introduce students to open-endedness we provide them the means "to orient themselves in the world through an understanding of acts of knowing and valuing that is more than intellectual and philosophical. It is a moral endeavor in the most personal sense" (1970, p. 54). There is more to liberal learning, as Perry alludes, than content mastery. When students encounter the incongruities inherent in liberal learning through the ill-structured problems that we design, they are faced with challenges to their attitudes, beliefs, and values. These problems hold the potential to take students to the edge where the familiar and the unusual meet.

In this intersection, students can experience liberal learning speaking to their lives. They can experience colleges and universities as learning resources, assemblages of people, books, laboratories, and an environment of things, ideas, passions, and ideals to be orchestrated by them to challenge and help them rethink their personal commitments to education and their capacity for human experience.

Note

*I have chosen William Perry because his work has been seminal to the field and his model echoes through the works of other scholars and studies. As important, his work seems to hold across gender and ethnic boundaries. For example, Carol Gilligan (1982) points out that the difference between men and women is not in how Perry's model outlines developmental transition, but that men and women move through what could be called different types of socially influenced personal paradigms (p. 165).

References

Association of American Colleges and Universities. *Statement on Liberal Learning, 1998.* http://www.aacuedu.org/About/statements/liberal_learning.cfm. Accessed Oct. 2004.

Bloom, A. *The Closing of the American Mind.* New York: Simon and Schuster, 1987.

Burch, K. "PBL, Politics, and Democracy." In B. Duch, S. Groh, and D. E. Allen (eds.), *The Power of Problem-Based Learning.* Sterling, Va.: Stylus, 2001.

Geertz, C. *The Interpretation of Cultures.* New York: Basic Books, 1973.

Gilligan, C. "Moral Development." In A. W. Chickering and Associates (eds.), *The Modern American College.* San Francisco: Jossey-Bass, 1981.

Gilligan, C. *In a Different Voice: Psychological Theory and Women's Development.* Cambridge, Mass.: Harvard University Press, 1982.

Graff, G. *Beyond the Culture Wars: How Teaching the Conflicts Can Revitalize American Education.* New York: Norton, 1992.

Graff, G. *Clueless in Academe: How Schooling Obscures the Life of the Mind.* New Haven: Yale University Press, 2003.

Kuhn, T. S. *The Structure of Scientific Revolutions.* Chicago: University of Chicago Press, 1970. (Originally published 1962)

Lakoff, G., and Johnson, M. *The Metaphors We Live By.* Chicago: University of Chicago Press, 1980.

Nussbaum, M. *Cultivating Humanity: A Classical Defense of Reform in Liberal Education.* Cambridge, Mass.: Harvard University Press, 1997.

Perry, W. G., Jr. *Forms of Intellectual and Ethical Development in the College Years: A Scheme.* Austin, Tex.: Holt, Rinehart, and Winston, 1970.

Rosenblatt, L. *Literature as Exploration.* New York: Modern Language Association, 1995.

Schneider, C. G. "Using Assessment to Focus Students and Departments on Goals Across the Curriculum." Paper presented at the Association of General and Liberal Studies, Kansas City, Nov. 13, 2004.

Scholes, R. *Textual Power: Literary Theory and the Teaching of English.* New Haven: Yale University Press, 1985.

NED SCOTT LAFF is coordinator for special academic projects and coordinator for core advising in the Office of the Provost at Loyola University Chicago.

2

Applying reading and writing theory to cases in composition, this chapter troubleshoots assignments that produced disappointing results and illustrates how the model of the "ill-structured problem" can help writing instructors craft assignments that foster the cognitive and affective maturation essential to college-level literacy.

Fostering Critical Literacy: The Art of Assignment Design

Arlene Wilner

Four decades ago, Booth (1963) lamented the artificiality of writing pedagogy, with its emphasis on "avoiding mistakes" rather than striving to say something interesting (p. 267). And while the mature Booth was able to sympathize with English teachers who are "bored silly" by piles of stultifying student papers, he argued that the torture was largely "self-inflicted" (p. 268). The remedy Booth suggested was—and is—simple in conception and very complex in practice. The best way to avoid the meaninglessness of typical freshman essays, he said, is to foster intellectual and moral maturation. And the best way to do that, he suggested, is to help students learn to read complex, narratively challenging texts: "We can subject our students to models of genuine narration, with the sharp observation and penetrating critical judgment that underlie all good story telling, whether reportorial or fictional. . . . A steady exposure to such voices is the very thing that will produce the maturity that alone can make our students ashamed of beclouded, commercial, borrowed spectacles for viewing the world" (pp. 503–504).

Central among teaching strategies in all courses that foster what Booth calls "discipline in reasoned argument, and . . . habits of addressing a living audience" (p. 504) is assignment design (Walvoord, 1998; Wiggins and McTighe, 1998). There are no formulas for crafting effective assignments,

---

A version of this chapter appeared as an article, "Asking for It: The Role of Assignment Design in Critical Literacy," in *Reader: Essays in Theory, Criticism, and Pedagogy, 52,* Spring 2005, 56–91.

but understanding the subtleties of the reading-writing connection suggested by Booth can help.

In the argument that follows, I hope to illuminate how the conception of an assignment as an "ill-structured problem" can address students' developmental needs, nurturing better reading and more authentic writing. In so doing, I want to illustrate how our assignments construct, in ways not always evident to us, our students' interactions with texts as both readers and authors.

The Model of Ill-Structured Problems

At best, the art of designing assignments is an engaging and deliberative process, not much different from the development we hope to nurture in students. It means figuring out how to ask for what we want lest we get what we ask for. Our assignments inevitably offer tacit information about what is worth asking and how one might go about developing answers. Preemptive measures that both anticipate naive approaches and improve the likelihood that students will be prompted to develop responses that expand the boundaries of their habitual thinking are thus worthy of more attention. Our success will depend on the level of awareness we bring to the task of reading selection and assignment design and on the richness of our repertoire for helping students achieve the necessary meld of personal engagement and critical distance. Bean (1996) has aptly summarized the advice of many critical-thinking theorists in asserting that the primary tasks for teachers are to create cognitive dissonance for students, to present knowledge as dynamic and dialogic, and to create opportunities for learning through active problem solving. In this context, he notes the efficacy of developing good "ill-structured" problems for students to wrestle with (p. 3).

Developed by researchers in information processing and, especially, artificial intelligence, the concept of *structure* in problems has been applied to the domain of critical thinking and pedagogy, usually within the context of expert versus novice practices. Ill-structured problems are pedagogically "good"; that is, because they are rooted in uncertainty and, often, ambiguity, they are not mere school exercises that test factual knowledge, but authentic questions, their solutions dependent on the kinds of thought processes that real-world practitioners engage in. Whereas well-structured problems tend to have an implied script or easily applied formula that leads to a particular solution that is testable and replicable, ill-structured ones require evaluation of a number of approaches, careful consideration of evidence, imagination of counterarguments, and the integration of information, concepts, and contexts, including those conditioned by values and attitudes (King and Kitchener, 1994; Petraglia, 1998; Voss, 1989). Different disciplines are interpreted by students as having more or less well-structured problems.

This disciplinary distinction became vividly apparent several years ago in a study I conducted to compare students' expectations with instructors' assumptions in introductory courses. I asked ten instructors to help me administer early in the semester the essay portion of the Measure of Intellectual Development,[1] which asks freshmen to reflect on what they consider their best learning experience in high school, specifying why the selected class worked so well for them. Of the trends that emerged, one is particularly relevant to assignment design: Although all students appreciate instructional strategies that make learning fun and respond to a sense that the teacher cares about them personally, they don't expect the same level of intellectual demand in all disciplines. Students apparently anticipate either well-structured problems (math and science classes) or no real problems in terms of structure (social science and humanities) but rather occasions for expression of opinion as an end in itself.

Student Development and Critical Literacy

The limitations and dangers of student (mis)understanding of disciplinary epistemologies are clear. Influential theorists like Louise Rosenblatt and Peter Elbow, who valorize the affective domain as a source of insight, nonetheless emphasize the importance of achieving mastery of the criteria that shape the "hierarchy of concepts" in disciplines (Elbow, 1986, p. 34). Rosenblatt's focus (1994) on the need for the student to choose a stance in relation to a given text suggests the self-awareness, and the awareness of interpretive strategies, necessary for a critical perspective. Research suggests that in high school, English classes in particular invite students to see the study of literature not as an opportunity for initiation into complex ways of reading and understanding multivocal texts and for the development of criteria for evaluation, but as an occasion for what appears to be deepened self-awareness based on reflexive responses (Langer, 1994).

As Rabinowitz, building on Rosenblatt's analysis, has reminded us, such "insights" remain static and shallow because they allow students to avoid real engagement with the text (Rabinowitz and Smith, 1998). However, as Rabinowitz and Smith have shown, developing teaching strategies that engage students in practicing the rules of the game is not necessarily intuitive, as such development requires a raised consciousness of what, for expert readers, is normally tacit understanding. The consequences of allowing expert practices to remain unarticulated can be significant. Curricula that fail to emphasize the nature of, and methodologies for solving, ill-structured problems appear to reinforce students' perception that complex questions are, or should be, reducible to simple answers and that questions to which there is no clearly right or wrong answer are entirely subject to the force of unexamined individual opinion.

If we view the attitudes expressed by students of high school age through the lens of the scheme developed by Perry in his now classic study of Harvard undergraduate students, *Forms of Intellectual and Ethical Development in the College Years* (1970), we can think more intentionally about how to develop effective literacy pedagogies by focusing on the problem-posing qualities of assignment design. Perry identifies nine "positions," ranging from a simplistic right-wrong view of knowledge through an acceptance of the contingent nature of understanding and an ability to make intellectual and ethical commitments within a relativist epistemology.[2] Perry's scheme posits Dualism—a belief in absolute truth—as epistemologically prior to Multiplicity, but as his own data made clear, these epistemologies usually exist side by side. The student's reliance on one or the other epistemology will depend on whether the question or problem is perceived to have a single correct answer or solution, that is, whether it is "well-structured." In the domains where emphasis is on discussion and point of view (what might be called non-problem-solving classes), the democracy of individual opinion generally prevails.

Elbow (1986) and Booth (1998) invoke the importance in critical reading of holding in a productive tension multiple layers of response. Rabinowitz and Smith (1998) emphasize the importance of training students to play the role of both authorial audience ("a hypothetical construction of what the author expects his or her readers to be like") and the narrative audience ("an imaginative creation by the author—something he or she hopes to convince the readers to pretend to become") (p. 23). All of these critics agree that, as Rabinowitz puts it, "intelligent reading involves a delicate and complex balancing act" that involves juggling multiple readerly roles (p. 28).

From Reading to Writing

The nature of the text, when read critically as both closed and open, constrained and liberating, affirmative and transformative, is also characteristic of writing assignments conceived as ill-structured problems. As Rosenblatt (1989) has reminded us, the texts our students produce also have implied authors, whose assumptions about their subject and their audience will determine their rhetorical stance. Comparing readers and writers, she points to the need for multiple interactions with one's own evolving text, including attention to its internal consistency ("a growing but often tacit sense of purpose") and a sense of its likely effect on a reader who is not the self (p. 167). The construction of a writerly self, like that of a readerly self, requires simultaneous sensitivity to one's own (developing) identity and an imagined other. In the examples that follow, I hope to illustrate how consciousness of the complexity of the reading-writing connection can help us to unpack our unexamined assumptions regarding how students read not only assigned texts but also the writing prompts aimed at engaging them more fully in those texts.

Example 1. An Ill-Structured Problem with Mixed-Message Instructions. The following prompt was included in a Research Writing course, the second half of the freshman composition sequence, in which a documented paper is required. The assignment elaborates the textbook editor's instructions for developing a conversation with a reading by either countering or extending the writer's argument:

> Your second essay is a single-source essay between 500 and 750 words. Choose one of the following three essays from *Writing from Sources* [ed. Brenda Spatt]: Charles Lindholm's "Love as an Experience of Transcendence (p. 172); Conque Henderson's "Myths of the Unloved" (p. 482); or Benjamin DeMott's "Visions of Black-White Friendship" (p. 531). Next, decide whether your strategy will be to argue against the essay or to develop an essay based on the essay. Both strategies are explained and discussed in *Writing from Sources* in chapter three.
>
> For your audience, imagine that you are writing your essay to be included in an anthology of essays by university students from around the country. In developing your strategy and your thesis, aim for a level of depth and sophistication that will challenge your readers to take a deeper look at the issues and themes presented in your selected essay.
>
> Approximately one-third of your grade for this essay will be based on your use of language: diction, grammar, and punctuation. The remainder of your grade will be determined by how well-organized, thoughtful, and persuasive your essay is—as well as by how you apply your strategy.

To its credit, rather than merely inviting unreflective opinions, this assignment requires, in preparation for research writing, participation in a dialogue with the text. Such a dialogue requires noticing contexts and purposes of the texts being engaged, as well as the meaningfulness of the issues. Thus, this prompt—in requiring selection of an argumentative stance (a "strategy" for response), in referring students to textbook instructions for carrying out the strategy, and in specifying an audience and purpose—has some essential attributes of a good ill-structured problem.

An experienced colleague who read the resulting set of student essays summed up its positive attributes, including its revelation of whether students had digested the original argument: "The assignment does invite and measure the target skills for English composition: college-level reading comprehension, critical thinking about texts, effective marshaling of evidence, engagement. [Moreover,] it sorts out relative student success effectively. . . . The student responses to the assignment break fairly dramatically into two groups. . . . Students who do not understand so as to be able to summarize the focal texts cannot successfully argue against or extend the original argument" (Hoff, letter to the author, July 2001). In fact, five of the twelve responses reflected serious misrepresentations of the chosen article.

Interestingly, all of the relatively unsuccessful student essays appeared to be attempts to extend rather than refute the article's thesis.

Part of the problem seems to have been the instructions offered by the textbook, which, I wish to argue, inadvertently invited the unsatisfactory responses noted above by allowing weaker readers to avoid a serious effort to engage the ideas in the selected text. The textbook's instructions for arguing against the source required a summary as the first step in writing the paper, whereas the instructions for "developing an essay based on the source" had a different emphasis: "This strategy gives you the freedom to develop your own ideas and present your own point of view in an essay that is only loosely linked to the source. Reading an assigned essay helps you to generate ideas and topics and provides you with evidence or information to cite in your own essay; but *the thesis, scope and organization of your essay are entirely your own* (Spatt, 1999, p. 159; emphasis in original).

Although students are asked several pages later to "*strive for an appropriate balance between your own ideas and those of your source*" (p. 165; emphasis in original), they may find the two instructions contradictory and naturally opt for the one that seems to offer more freedom.

Moreover, the guidelines for writing an argument against the source are significantly simpler and fewer (that is, present and analyze the source's view, then present your own position) than the rather elaborate twelve-point list offered for developing a topic based on the source, including the need for brainstorming (a process to which three pages of text are dedicated) to find a topic in the first place. This emphasis encourages students to consider topic-definition to be the main challenge of the extension or development option rather than evidence of engagement with the original argument.

Thus, while the instructor's assignment itself has the marks of a good ill-structured problem, one of the two textbook strategies presented to students contains some potential contradictions and complications that increase the risk of inadequate performance, especially for students whose reading skills are relatively weak. I would suspect that students who choose to develop, rather than counter, the point of an essay would require substantial coaching to begin to establish the kind of partnership that the textbook editor offers as a metaphor for the relationship between the voice of the selected essay and one's own voice: "*All of the important positions in the structure of your essay should be filled by you.* . . . On the other hand, the reader should not be allowed to lose sight of the source essay; it should be treated as a form of evidence and cited whenever it is relevant, but always as a context in which to develop your own strategy and assert your own thesis" (p. 165; emphasis in original). This kind of partnership is precisely the relationship that underlies development of the so-called research paper typically assigned at the end of the freshman year—and most freshman-writing instructors would agree that it is rarely achieved in the way we hope. Hence the importance of composing and supporting assignments that are ill-structured problems that ask students to practice, holistically, the integrated skill set they need to develop.

The complexity of this skill set is, I believe, often underestimated. In their discussions of critical pedagogies, researchers have reminded us of the many (usually tacit) skills implicit in the reading required for college courses. The following case analysis illustrates how this complex of challenges informs students' responses to a synthesis assignment, how the flaws in the assignment serve to inhibit rather than enhance critical reading and persuasive writing, and what some alternative writing prompts might look like.

Example 2. An "Insoluble" Ill-Structured Problem. Below is the first assignment in a section of Research Writing, the second or third course in a two- to three-semester composition sequence (depending on initial placement). The instructor of this section, a talented graduate student, had already proven to be unusually thoughtful in designing syllabi and prompts, revising and refining them by taking guidance from the qualities of students' responses. Sensitive to students' need for preparation of various kinds, she was always careful to "lay the groundwork for discussions regarding how to write an argument, construct an original and meaningful thesis, [and] synthesize information/ideas from diverse texts" (instructor's course portfolio). In this instance, however, the results were especially disappointing, and it was hard to say why.

The Assignment:

> Both Engelmann's "Two Germans" [McCuen and Winkler, 1991, pp. 497–551] and Sophocles' *Antigone* address the necessity of viewing an idea or issue from more than one point of view or perspective. And both works demonstrate the possibly dire effects that can result from persisting in a narrow or one-sided point of view. Drawing upon the stated and implied ideas presented in "Two Germans" and *Antigone,* explore possible reasons for Herr Berger's, Antigone's, and Creon's narrow-mindedness (for example, were their views rooted in any laudable ideal?) and the consequences of their perspective—both to themselves, others, and the community in general. Consider the role that intermediaries like Ismene and the narrator/editor in "Two Germans" play. To what extent, if any, are they able to shape or amend the one-sidedness of others' views?

("Two Germans" is an anthologized excerpt from a book by journalist Bernt Engelmann, a World War II Luftwaffe radio operator who became a resistor and was imprisoned in Dachau. The book, *In Hitler's Germany* (1985), is based on interviews that detail the German resistance movement. Engelmann's interview with Irene, sole survivor of her family, and with Herr Berger, a former Gestapo agent, comprise the excerpt assigned to the students.)

The Responses. The following representative observations from students' papers suggest the lower level of the Perry scale, mainly Multiplicity

Diffuse—recognition that individuals have "different sides," that a shift in perspective might lead to a different judgment of a person or an event, that it is ethically admirable to try to see a point of view other than one's own, and that refusal to do so ("narrow-mindedness" in the terms of the assignment) is a bad quality that is bound to have negative effects. Tellingly, most students appeared to miss or to disregard a crucial hint offered under "Reading Advice" from the editors of the anthology: "That the Gestapo agent has absolutely no compunction about his past is a source of both horror and dramatic tension" (McCuen and Winkler, 1991, p. 498). Neither horror nor tension is at all apparent in students' responses; instead, they try mightily to be "fair and balanced," avoiding not only judgmentalism, but judgment of any kind:

> Automatically there is a negative opinion of Herr Berger for the simple fact he participated in the Holocaust. However, through the narrator's words, one can see the other side of the story and another side of a person.
> Both stories display an array of opinions that can be sided with either way.
> Each story has a variation of ideas behind it. They both show people with different beliefs and values.
> Herr Berger believes that what he did was right, while Engelmann believes that the lifestyle Berger led was a disgrace. In the end, whose point of view is right and whose is wrong?
> In "Two Germans" the narrator is the open-minded one. He tries to look at both sides of the story, and listen to what both characters have to say.
> By reading these two works, you learn that not only should a person try to look at other points of view, but also see what the consequences could be if you continue to be selfish in your judgments.

These reactions reveal that the assignment, although it seems to have the complexity and open-endedness of an ill-structured problem, actually has an implicit thesis—that Antigone, Creon, and Herr Berger all manifest a "one-sidedness" or "narrow-mindedness" that results in destructive consequences for themselves and others.

The instructor's intention was to prompt a consideration of the importance of perspective in the determination of ethical judgments (that is, to complicate the students' view of right and wrong); however, the terms of the assignment, she could see in retrospect, invited students to assimilate complex ideas to familiar and simplistic ways of thinking. For example, students praised Engelmann for his open-mindedness in listening politely both to the self-justifying Nazi officer and the Holocaust survivor, as if these voices were intended to carry equal moral weight. For these students, "open-mindedness" meant refusing to value commitment to principle in favor of finding the mean between extremes—even when no such compromise is available because the positions are predicated on antithetical value systems and even when one of the extremes is clearly vicious.

Unpacking the Challenges. In an interview on teaching freshman composition, the instructor reflected on the gap between her intentions and students' understanding of their task:

> We were reading a background source—*Antigone and Its Moral* by George Eliot and . . . her argument basically said something to the effect that Antigone and Creon represent warring halves of human nature, one that's very much interested in family and pursuing a faith and belief in the gods and another that's more secular and more public-minded, and that, although neither of these viewpoints is wrong, that's what makes *Antigone* such a rich play—they're both right. However, they can't acknowledge or see the other point of view, or if they do realize that it's there, which they do, they choose to ignore it and stand by their own beliefs.
>
> . . . I ended up with somewhat reductive responses from the students in essay form—Creon's narrow-mindedness, etc. And, in many cases they neglected the nuanced point that, in at least Antigone and Creon's case, they're both right as well as both wrong, and not as much was made of that controversy or that tension between the characters themselves and between the belief systems that were being represented. . . . Both Engelmann and Sophocles addressed the necessity of viewing an idea or issue from more than one point of view or perspective and both works demonstrate the possibly dire effects that result if one continues to stand by the one point of view.

Through this reflection, one begins to understand the evolution of the fault lines in the assignment. While one could argue that Antigone and Creon are "both right" (although many students struggled with this ambiguity), one could hardly say the same for the two Germans. But that is what students, based on their reading of the assignment, thought they had to argue.

In pondering the gap between pedagogic intention and student performance, the instructor and I considered the complex of skills students would need to approach the assignment successfully.

Understanding text rhetoric. What *Antigone* demands rhetorically is both an understanding of the tension between two legitimately competing worldviews represented by Antigone and Creon, respectively, and of the enormous difficulty, for one entrusted with the public welfare in wartime, of balancing individual rights with public security. The failure of the public figure to strike the proper balance in response to an emergent occasion results in both personal tragedy and civic disorder.

Engelmann's piece, emerging from a very different context, derives its power from a deeply disturbing trio of voices that defy accommodation: the chillingly detailed testimony of Holocaust survivor Irene Herz; the selective and self-justifying recollections of an SS officer; and the interjected comments of the interviewer, Engelmann, who was himself a key character in the story being witnessed.

The assignment offers insight into the ways it might play into the novice habits of students. If each character is assumed to be "one-sided," then there is no point in trying to tease out contradictions within them. This model, wrested from the text through a strained analogy with *Antigone*, allows students to see the assignment as a well-structured problem (apply the lessons of *Antigone* to "Two Germans") and thus to lapse into commonplaces that have little to do with "Two Germans." Moreover, the implied thesis is itself seductive in its apparent simplicity—compromise is preferable to stubbornness.

Understanding genre. In addition to considering each author's position in relation to his text, students could be encouraged to see that the two texts demand rather different readerly stances. Such an awareness would "require knowing the genre in which the authorial audience places the text" (Rabinowitz and Smith, 1998, p. 63).

In comparing Sophocles's text with Engelmann's, one would need to sense, for example, the difference between, on the one hand, the mythic and ritualistic (hence conservative) aspects of an ancient Greek tragedy performed before an audience that already knows the story and the conventions through which it will be portrayed and, on the other, the subtle, nervous suspense implicit in a journalistic report of a war criminal's attitude toward an earlier version of himself (in what ways will he evade confronting the moral meanings of this self). Moreover, Engelmann depends on the reader's automatic recognition of Berger's revolting capacity for cruelty and his enduring moral hollowness, a quality quite different from the arc through which Sophocles reveals Creon's character and effects the catharsis of tragedy.

Recognizing Authentic Engagement

Even when we unwittingly craft assignments that tend to lead our students down an undesirable path, we may nonetheless be rewarded by instances of student insight that can give us clues about what we might have done better. In this case, it was gratifying to notice some essays that transcended the boundaries of a reductive reading. Consider, for example, how the student who wrote the following passage redefined the terms of the prompt: "Being narrow-minded or stubborn are two characteristics that may sometimes be viewed as positive if one uses the words 'focused' and 'determined.' But they may also be dangerous and, therefore, cause many outrageous and negative incidents by being taken too far. The three characters, Antigone, Creon, and Herr Berger, all possess this trait for being single-minded and have to suffer much distress in their lives because of their strong, willful, and unvarying beliefs and values."

What does it mean to "take [these qualities] too far"? Encouraged to pursue the question, implicit in her own comments, of how commitment can be either "positive" or "dangerous," depending on underlying values and contexts, this student might have been led to make some crucial distinctions that are glossed over in her concluding sentence.

Another student revealed her awareness of the incommensurate nature of the two texts by peppering her observations on Berger and his actions with fittingly graphic adjectives—"gruesome," "hideous," "horrible," "inhuman"—demonstrating the opposite of the detached balance and objectivity most of her classmates felt obliged to endorse. Although this student finally argued for the strained analogy apparently required, claiming—to the instructor's frustration—that Herr Berger and Antigone "exhibit the same characteristics of narrow-mindedness ending in tragedy," her unflinching judgment of one character's behavior as barbarous might fuel a useful class discussion.

The Text and "I"

I have been suggesting that although we may not like what we get from students, we need to consider whether what we get is in fact what we have unwittingly asked for and whether some institutionalized pedagogies work at cross-purposes with our goals. Rosenblatt (1989) is, I believe, correct in her assessment that "Many current teaching practices—the kinds of questions asked, the way assignments are phrased, the types of tests given, the atmosphere created in the classroom—counteract the very processes presumably being taught and foster manipulations of empty abstractions" (p. 172). If we are disturbed that the majority of students who chose the Antigone/Engelmann topic appeared to remain so coolly disengaged from the questions it raises, satisfied to respond to an emotionally harrowing narrative with clichés about how "a person should try to look at other points of view," we might consider the contexts that foster such detachment.

In a comparison of high-school pedagogic philosophy and strategies across four disciplines—biology, physics, history, and literature—Langer (1994) found that only literature classes privileged students' responses over the course content. While none of the classes included explicit instruction or practice in disciplinary epistemologies, and while all implied somewhat different philosophies in methods of question-posing and problem solving, the English classes were unique in their lack of attention to information and their focus on individual response. Unlike the teachers of the other disciplines, the English teachers "assumed that the essential meaning was in their students, based on the life experiences they had engaged in or witnessed" (p. 96). In one of the literature classes studied, "the students' responses were often treated as more important than the text" (p. 104).

These findings are consistent with the distinctions among students' descriptions of their best high school learning experience. In "soft" science or humanities subjects—fields that resist transmission through well-structured problems—the feelings generated by the class (for example, the sense that all opinions are equally valuable, the inclusiveness of open-ended discussion unbounded by the need to develop criteria for evaluation of one position versus another) can have the effect of relegating the subject matter itself into a shadow zone, with unreflective responses and opinions in the foreground. Somewhat paradoxically (in view of this emphasis), high school students are often instructed to avoid using "I" in their academic essays. It is a striking irony that the same students who feel encouraged to believe that it is their unexamined opinions that matter most are enjoined from identifying their subjectivity when writing a formal essay. The misperception that academic writing is devoid of personal voice is perhaps an effect of the "fact-value" split—the reluctance to assert meaningful criteria for evaluation—discussed by Booth (1988, p. 28).

Most of us would probably accept that the invocation of feeling is not only legitimate but necessary to critical reading. But how many of us remind ourselves that this understanding is counter to the common belief among students that good academic writing maintains a neutral and thus a "fair" stance toward the material? As McCormick (1990) has observed, students who are taught that academic writing necessarily excludes the first person singular often believe "that they can best succeed in school by ignoring rather than developing their ideas" (p. 197). Such "effacement of subjectivity" (Spellmeyer, 1989, p. 265) hinders the development of an authentic voice.

When asked why the use of first-person singular is generally forbidden in formal essays, students cite a range of reasons reflecting their novice position, including the need to avoid the appearance of bias and the reluctance of teachers to grade their students' point of view. The truth, rarely articulated by teachers, is that students who use "I think," "I believe," or—as is commonly the case—"I feel," are generally producing unprocessed opinions or emotional responses unshaped by analysis or by attention to the constraints of the text or context to which the opinion is a response. The result of the rule, then, is to encourage the surface appearance of academic discourse without fostering the rigorous engagement and consequent conviction that underlie authentic communication.

What to Ask For

What sorts of questions about the Sophocles and Engelmann texts, then, might draw students closer to the worlds of those writers and at the same time help them extend the text into the world of ideas and into the world of their felt experience? Concurring with Jerome Bruner (1996) that "good questions are ones that pose dilemmas, subvert obvious or canonical 'truths,' [and] force incongruities upon our attention" (p. 127), I present the following as examples of the kinds of questions likely to encourage engaged reading and authentic writing.

Assignment

Given the following context, write a four-page essay on one of the topics below.

Context: Sophocles's *Antigone* (an ancient Greek drama performed as part of a theater competition in Athens c. 441 BC) and Bernt Engelmann's "Two Germans" (an excerpt from a book by a Nazi resister who had been imprisoned in a concentration camp during WWII) each give voice to perspectives that are diametrically opposed to each other, and both portray great violence and suffering as a result of the conflict.

Sample Topics: The virtues of compromise are often touted. When two perspectives clash, is compromise always possible? Is it always desirable? Drawing on the events portrayed in *Antigone* and "Two Germans," explore the idea of compromise from the perspectives of both practicality and morality. Keep in mind historical contexts, especially realistic options for the various characters in their respective times, places, and social-political situations.

Explore the concept of *guilt* in *Antigone* and "Two Germans" by comparing the nature of Antigone's and Creon's behavior with Herr Berger's. Who is guilty of what and why? In your argument, consider how the author's presentation and ordering of information affects your evaluation. (Some questions you may find helpful to your thinking: Is the reader encouraged to think that the guilt of the individual in each case is mitigated by circumstance and dependent on perspective or does it seem absolute? In what ways do the individuals assume, or fail to assume, responsibility for their actions? In what ways does the outcome in each case suggest that justice has or has not been served? If not, what would have been a just outcome?)

In asking students to write in response to such topics, we are modeling the kinds of questions we think it is important to ask. The form of the ill-structured problem—a kind of bounded openness—is intended to help students use the tools of the discipline while moving beyond gamesmanship into an authentic response, if not yet a mature commitment. Holding students accountable to the terms of such assignments would not, of course, guarantee excellent results, but it would position students within classic and ongoing conversations about issues that, in the realpolitik that informs civic discourse and policymaking, have concrete consequences for their lives.

Although none of these questions leads to a definitive answer, neither do they allow for equally simplistic open-endedness. The comfortingly "democratic" paradigm (Perry's lower levels of Multiplicity, what Craig E. Nelson (1999, p. 48) has called the "Baskin-Robbins" level of thinking, in which all flavors are good and there is no way to determine that one is "better" than another) simply will not serve when problems like these must be addressed.

Conclusion

Since purposeful assignment design can play an essential role in evoking complex transactions with texts, students benefit when instructors are more attentive to this essential aspect of pedagogy. Usually, the real rules of engagement—the development of shared criteria for evaluation, an awareness of the constraints imposed by genre, an understanding of how to critique texts while simultaneously being persuaded by them—remain tacit because they are not easily teachable; too often we are sabotaged by our own expertise, crafting assignments that invite, from our novice students, responses counter to our purposes. In my experience as a composition workshop facilitator, collaborative peer review of assignments can yield striking insights, as colleagues help each other see with fresh eyes how the balance between challenge and support might be improved.

In formulating the questions above, I have tried to imagine students both comprehending the texts sufficiently to enjoy them and also being pressured to "resist the very texts from which they derive textual pleasure: to analyze, to dissect, and to oppose," an expertise that Scholes (1985) considers "the great aim or end of liberal education" (p. 62). While acknowledging with Bartholomae (1995) that students must be instructed in critical reading (p. 65), we must also heed Elbow's reminder (1995) that effective writing can issue only from someone who has something meaningful to say and feels motivated to say it. Certainly the data underlying my argument are given point by Elbow's distinction between the role of academic student writer (writing to get it "right," to please the teacher) and the role of (genuine) writer: "The basic subtext in a piece of student writing is likely to be, 'Is this okay?' In contrast to students, the basic subtext in a writer's text is likely to be, 'Listen to me, I have something to tell you.'" (p. 81).

This distinction is exemplified in the responses to the Sophocles-Engelmann assignment, in which thoughtful, genuine voices are discernible through the haze of clichés. At these breakthrough moments, authorized reading (Rabinowitz and Smith, 1998) is evident in authorized writing. Pedagogic strategies for enabling this dynamic are, as I have been arguing, neither simple nor especially efficient. Indeed, as all of the critics whose voices I have engaged here would agree, we are confronted with a paradox: In order to nurture authenticity in students' voices, we need to help them incorporate—through a combination of openness and resistance—other voices first. Since showing them how to do that is itself an ill-structured problem, shouldn't we be seeking more opportunities to work together on it?

Notes

1. Research for this study was supported by a grant from the Carnegie Academy for the Scholarship of Teaching and Learning. I am grateful to Michele Haughey, Katharine Hoff, Beth Meszaros, and Liam Quirk, dedicated teacher-scholars, whose generous participation with me in classroom research enabled this project, and to my outstanding student collaborators—Alexandra Alazio, Natasha Gwira, Tymish Halibey, and Jay Imbrenda—who helped teach me what to ask for. My additional thanks to Dr. William S. Moore, of the Center for the Study of Intellectual Development/The Perry Network (Olympia, Wash.), for permission to share samples of students' responses.

2. Perry's scheme has prompted a number of related studies that have helped to refine and extend his theories. Reviewers have found that despite their different emphases, these studies share Perry's view of the "general trend of development" from a view of knowledge as right or wrong to an acceptance of relativism and then to a view of "individuals as active constructors of meaning, able to make judgments and commitments in a relativistic context" (Hofer and Pintrich, 1997, p. 121). See also William S. Moore, "Student and Faculty Epistemology in the College Classroom: The Perry Schema of Intellectual and Ethical Development" (1994).

References

Bartholomae, D. "Writing with Teachers: A Conversation with Peter Elbow." *College Composition and Communication,* 1995, *46*(1), 62–71.

Bean, J. *Engaging Ideas: The Professor's Guide to Integrating Writing, Critical Thinking, and Active Learning in the Classroom.* San Francisco: Jossey-Bass, 1996.

Booth, W. C. *The Company We Keep: An Ethics of Fiction.* Berkeley: University of California Press, 1988.

Booth, W. C. "The Ethics of Teaching Literature." *College English,* Sept. 1998, *61* (1), 41–55.

Booth, W. C. "Boring from Within: The Art of the Freshman Essay." (Adapted from a speech to the Illinois Council of College Teachers of English, 1963.) In L. H. Eastman, J. C. Betreton, and J. E. Hartman (eds.), *The Norton Reader: An Anthology of Nonfiction Prose.* (10th ed.) New York: Norton, 2000.

Bruner, J. *The Culture of Education.* Cambridge, Mass.: Harvard University Press, 1996.

Elbow, P. *Embracing Contraries: Explorations in Learning and Teaching.* New York: Oxford University Press, 1986.

Elbow, P. "Being a Writer vs. Being an Academic: A Conflict of Goals." *College Composition and Communication,* 1995, *46*(1), 72–83.

Eliot, G. "The Antigone and Its Moral" (1856). In T. Pinney (ed.), *Essays of George Eliot.* New York: Columbia University Press, 1963.

Engelmann, B. "Two Germans." In J. R. McCuen and A. C. Winkler (eds.), *Reading, Writing, and the Humanities.* Orlando: Harcourt Brace, 1991.

Hofer, B. K., and Pintrich, P. R. "The Development of Epistemological Theories: Beliefs about Knowledge and Knowing and Their Relation to Learning." *Review of Educational Research,* 1997, *67*(1), 88–140.

King, P. M., and Strohm Kitchener, K. *Developing Reflective Judgment: Understanding and Promoting Intellectual Growth and Critical Thinking in Adolescents and Adults.* San Francisco: Jossey-Bass, 1994.

Langer, J. A. "Teaching Disciplinary Thinking in Academic Coursework." In J. N. Mangieri and C. C. Block (eds.), *Creating Powerful Thinking in Teaching and Students: Diverse Perspectives.* Orlando: Harcourt Brace, 1994.

McCormick, K. "The Cultural Imperatives Underlying Cognitive Acts." In L. S. Flower and others (eds.), *Reading-to-Write: Exploring a Cognitive and Social Process.* New York: Oxford University Press, 1990.

McCuen, J. R., and Winkler, A. C. (eds.). *Reading, Writing, and the Humanities.* Orlando: Harcourt Brace, 1991.

Moore, W. S. "Student and Faculty Epistemology in the College Classroom: The Perry Schema of Intellectual and Ethical Development." In K. W. Pritchard and R. M. Sawyer (eds.), *Handbook of College Teaching.* Westport, Conn.: Greenwood Press, 1994.

Nelson, C. E. "On the Persistence of Unicorns: The Tradeoff Between Content and Critical Thinking Revisited." In B. A. Pescolido and R. Aminzade (eds.), *The Social*

Worlds of Higher Education: Handbook for Teaching in a New Century. Newbury Park, Calif.: Pine Forge Press, 1999.

Perry, W. G., Jr. *Forms of Intellectual and Ethical Development in the College Years: A Scheme.* Austin, Tex.: Holt, Rinehart, and Winston, 1970.

Petraglia, J. *Reality by Design: The Rhetoric and Technology of Authenticity in Education.* Mahwah, N.J.: Erlbaum, 1998.

Rabinowitz, P. J., and Smith, M. W. *Authorizing Readers: Resistance and Respect in the Teaching of Literature.* New York: Teachers College Press/National Council of Teachers of English, 1998.

Rosenblatt, L. M. "Writing and Reading: The Transactional Theory." In J. M. Mason (ed.), *Reading and Writing Connections.* Needham Heights, Mass.: Allyn & Bacon, 1989.

Rosenblatt, L. M. *The Reader, the Text, the Poem: The Transactional Theory of the Literary Work.* (rev. ed.) Carbondale: Southern Illinois University Press, 1994.

Scholes, R. *Textual Power: Literary Theory and the Teaching of English.* New Haven: Yale University Press, 1985.

Spatt, B. *Writing from Sources.* (5th ed.) New York: St. Martins Press, 1999.   •

Spellmeyer, K. "A Common Ground: The Essay in the Academy." *College English,* 1989, *51*(3), 262–276.

Voss, James F. "On the Composition of Experts and Novices." In E. P. Maimon, B. F. Nodine, and F. W. O'Connor (eds.), *Thinking, Reasoning, and Writing.* New York: Longman, 1989.

Walvoord, B. E., and Anderson, J. A. *Effective Grading: A Tool for Learning and Assessment.* San Francisco: Jossey-Bass, 1998.

Wiggins, G., and McTighe, J. *Understanding by Design.* Alexandria, Va.: Association for Supervision and Curriculum Development, 1998.

ARLENE WILNER *is professor of English at Rider University and director of BRIDGE (Bridging Research, Instruction, and Discipline-Grounded Epistemologies), a campuswide faculty-development program that supports the scholarship of teaching and learning.*

3

This chapter argues that the use of debates in a core world history course can foster both authentic learning in the discipline and progress toward intellectual and ethical maturity.

Debate and Student Development in the History Classroom

Anne Osborne

> The only way in which a human being can make some approach to knowing the whole of a subject, is by hearing what can be said about it by persons of every variety of opinion.
> –John Stuart Mill, 1859, p. 25

> You're doing theater, when you should be doing debate, which would be great. . . . What you do is not honest. What you do is partisan hackery.
> –Jon Stewart, *Crossfire*, October 15, 2004

Can student development, a sense of civic responsibility, and a sense of self be fostered through core history requirements? Does a focus on these goals distract from the fulfillment of disciplinary goals? Or is it possible that activities and assignments intended to foster student engagement and participation in "authentic" historical tasks will also provide opportunities for student development both as autonomous selves and as citizens? Are classroom debates a particularly useful technique in working toward the goals of a liberal arts education?

Note: Research for this project was supported by a summer fellowship from Rider University. I am grateful to Arlene Wilner and Katherine Hoff for generously sharing their expertise as well as to my fellow BRIDGE participants for their insights and encouragement.

Education in the liberal arts has at least three goals. The first is fulfill-ment of disciplinary goals. The second is the personal development of the student, intellectually, emotionally, and ethically. The third is the prepara-tion of the student, as a social and political being, to deal with others with tolerance and respect, with enough humility to recognize one's own human fallibility, yet with enough self-confidence to arrive at a personal commit-ment to a set of fundamental values or principles. These are challenging goals. Yet the undergraduate years should help the student progress in all these areas and should help to inculcate an interest and pleasure in the life of the mind that will allow that progress to continue throughout the stu-dent's lifetime.

In this chapter, I shall describe the pursuit of these goals in a history core course. After experimenting with various configurations of discussions and debates for several years, my conclusion is not only that the study of history can serve these broader developmental goals, but also that the same techniques that further the goals of personal development and preparation for citizenship can help students attain the disciplinary goals. In fact, I argue that classroom debates are a particularly effective way of working toward these goals.

History is an argument without end: in fact, academic culture in gen-eral is a culture of argumentation, and democracies are societies in which debate is central (Graff, 2003; Woodruff, 2004). Yet this culture of argu-ment is initially alien to most students. Thus debates help students learn to participate in the "academic conversation," and in turn in the public dis-course of our democratic society as well. Development in these areas not only makes them better students in the classroom, they also become better-prepared citizens. And by learning to argue effectively, they build up "forms of intellectual capital that have a lot of power in the world" (Graff, p. 9).

The Target Course

The course described here is the first half of the two-semester world history sequence required of all liberal arts students at Rider University. Students are mostly freshmen, non-majors, with little background and, initially, lit-tle interest. The very broad coverage mandated by the core requirement (the entire world from prehistory to 1500 CE) makes deep engagement with any particular culture or period difficult. Students, not surprisingly, tend to see history as a matter of memorizing facts rather than making arguments. Although they are able on the first day of class dutifully to articulate some reasons why the study of world history might be thought useful, they gen-erally find it difficult to see connections between these abstract goals and what they actually are doing to study world history.

The disciplinary goals for this class include the ability to analyze pri-mary sources, to understand and apply the historical method, and to see contemporary affairs in historical context, as well as the attainment of broad cultural literacy. The goals also include development of the student's ability to read and write critically and analytically.

Student development goals relate to the attainment of enough perspective for the student both to enter into an imaginative empathy with other cultures and to be able to question the seemingly self-evident perfection of our own.

Citizenship goals include development of the ability to debate and to reason. As Paul Woodruff argues in *First Democracy: The Challenge of an Ancient Idea,* commitment to democracy is grounded in a belief in the ability of ordinary citizens in the aggregate to have enough wisdom and enough capacity to reason to be able to make appropriate judgments even in the absence of specialized knowledge.

I would argue that the development of wisdom that allows us to make judgments in the absence of specialized knowledge is somewhat similar to the division between experts and novices analyzed by Sam Wineburg (2001). As he has shown, expertise in academic disciplines is not just a result of the accumulation of factual knowledge. Rather, it is the result of having developed patterns of thinking appropriate to the discipline that lead the expert to see patterns, ask questions, and anticipate possibilities even in the absence of a full command of the data, so that, as he demonstrated, historians who knew relatively little factual information about particular situations nonetheless were able to analyze those situations in sophisticated ways, while novices who had demonstrated much greater familiarity with detailed facts were less able to do so (see also National Research Council, 1999). This is not to argue that factual information is of no value: after all, the experts developed their sophisticated ways of thinking through their analysis of data in other contexts. But it suggests that it is possible to generalize from a sophisticated understanding of one context to apply those habits of mind in other contexts. If we are not to surrender control over our future to technocrats, active citizenship in a democracy requires the development of habits of mind that can perceive patterns, ask sophisticated questions, and anticipate possibilities even without detailed knowledge: it is more useful to know some things well and deeply than to acquire a superficial mastery of a broad array of facts.

Debate Goals

Several years ago, when I began to integrate a series of debates into the world history class, my initial goals were simple: I hoped that debates would engage student interest and would provide a context in which readings of primary sources and short works of scholarship would be relevant. I thought well-chosen readings would reinforce engagement with the class and that this would encourage compliance with these assignments.

Initiating students into the study of history by inviting them to debate is also more authentic than asking them to memorize facts or write essay exams. The aspect of the course that is closest to what historians actually do is the debates: reading, analyzing, evaluating both the work of scholars and the primary sources it is based on and using this study as the foundation to make arguments of their own is basically very similar to what historians do and also similar to the use one hopes they will make of history as citizens in the future. This approach would help students become more sophisticated historians (Walvoord and Breihan, 1990).

As the project developed, I realized that the questions for debate could be chosen not only with a view to exploring historically significant issues, making use of engaging scholarship and stimulating student interest, although these remained critical; they could also be chosen to encourage students to grapple with anomalies and challenge their own preconceptions. This experience in turn should reinforce their engagement. Thus the format of debate, in addition to fostering the attainment of disciplinary goals, could also drive students' personal development, contributing to what Ned Laff in Chapter One of this volume discusses as a personal "paradigm shift."

World history is full of examples of institutions, practices, and beliefs related to class, race, gender, power, and spirituality that differ radically from what most American adolescents in the early twenty-first century consider to be obviously natural. But this project did not envision a reversion to an older, discredited vision of history, as "philosophy teaching by example," in the famous dictum of Lord Bolingbroke; it was not to be a grab bag of neat little stories that could be followed by the moral, like Aesop's fables. Instead, the exploration of these challenging cases would have to be embedded in a study of the social and historical context in which these ideas or practices made sense and seemed as natural to the people of that time and place as elements of our culture do to us today. Thus the readings and discussions would contribute to the goal of developing the capacity to move beyond the dualistic assumption that there is a right and wrong answer to every question ("I'm right and you're an idiot") to understand other points of view. While the initial reaction might be lazy tolerance that refuses to address complexity ("It's all good"), that is at least a step forward from close-minded judgmentalism ("Burn in hell, heretic!"). Many students remain at this relativistic level (Colby, Ehrlich, Beaumont, and Stephens, 2003), but ideally, students would gradually develop the ability to move beyond relativism and distinguish among various propositions and to offer legitimate support to a personal stand, based on an understanding of those ideas and consciously committing to a set of values (Perry, 1970). It is possible that debating issues where students must confront arguments on both sides may help students mature in this way.

The questions could also have a fairly direct link of some kind with current events. In this way, the relevance of the issue and the readings would not just be self-contained within the class (do the readings or you will have nothing to say in the debate), but also would clearly relate to students' personal worlds or public issues. It would encourage the habit of mind of viewing current issues in a historical context. Mastery of information and of terms of debate on prominent issues could be empowering for students as well, thus providing yet another reason for students to get involved and reinforcement for those who did so.

As the nation began to gear up for the presidential election in the fall of 2003, and especially as campaigning accelerated in 2004, the deficiencies in the American culture of public discourse became ever more painfully apparent. In that context it seemed to me that another benefit that debates in college courses could offer is that students are asked to learn good intellectual habits that also enhance students' preparation as citizens. Debates encourage them to listen or read attentively, summarize accurately, reflect, take a clear stand, support that stand with evidence, and present their position effectively, including engaging with the opposing side by rebutting its counterarguments. As Graff (2003) points out, even crude debates can be a step in the right direction as long as they avoid attempts to score cheap points by misrepresenting opponents or by humiliating them rather than seriously engaging their ideas; in any case, such attacks are not true debates but rather, as Jon Stewart famously told his *Crossfire* hosts, are "partisan hackery" that on the national scene are hurtful to the country (Stewart, 2004).

For each debate I created a packet of primary sources and short pieces of historical scholarship. I also created a Blackboard on-line discussion thread. We analyzed the historical works in class and then debated the issue, using that material as evidence. Students wrote a short essay taking a stand on the issues we had debated. They also submitted related news reports to the on-line discussion and commented on their own and other students' submissions. Although the students were assigned a position in the debate, they were encouraged to take a personal stand in their papers, so they had the experience both of adopting and defending attitudes and values they may have disagreed with and the experience of defending a personal position with evidence.

A Concrete Example

The first debate I developed was "Women in Islam." It forces students to reevaluate common stereotypes of a monolithic and misogynistic Islam as well as to explore the contingent historical circumstances that shaped various practices. This experience fosters discussion of the variety of women's experiences in different Muslim cultures and encourages examination of students' own assumptions about modern American gender ideals as natural or inevitable. Beginning in 1999 I began having students read and discuss a chapter from Leila Ahmed's *Women and Gender in Islam: The Historical Roots of a Modern Debate* (1992). In that chapter, Ahmed explores the implications for women of the coming of Islam through examining the lives of two of the Prophet's wives: his first wife, Khadija, who was more than ten years his senior and who as a wealthy widow had employed him in her business and remained his only wife until her death; and Aisha, who married the Prophet when she was nine or ten years old and shared her position with many co-wives, although she was always considered to be his favorite. Ahmed analyzes the Qur'an and a number of *hadiths* (short narratives about the sayings and practices of the Prophet Muhammad and his Companions in the first generation of Islam, believed to be authentic oral traditions passed down in a chain of transmission from eye witnesses). She regards Islam as it developed historically as having severely circumscribed women's rights and women's lives. But her work makes clear that the interpretation that finds Qur'anic sanction for these limitations is not the only possible interpretation. Students were given the Ahmed text and asked to read the text at home and to identify the thesis, note the sources, and address the issue of the oral transmission of key information. In the following class or, often, two classes, students discussed the various texts in groups, then we opened it up to the whole class. The next class they debated. I asked them to come in with key points highlighted and to refer to particular passages of Ahmed's scholarship and to specific verses of the Qur'an or to specific actions or sayings of Muhammad to support the points they made in the debate. Finally, they wrote a short essay on the subject, using Ahmed's scholarship, the Qur'an, and the hadiths as evidence.

Before I adopted classroom debates, I had used this text as the basis for class discussion. I assumed that the personal nature of the subject—biographies of real individuals and an exploration of marriage in another culture—would be inherently interesting to the students. This proved to be true. When I tried to make it more engaging, and especially to engage all students, not just the most verbal, by converting the discussion into a debate, that required a question—ideally something relevant to the modern world, a question that the students could discuss with the evidence from Ahmed's book and from the Qur'an. So in August, 2001, as I prepared for the coming semester, I revised this assignment. I decided to make it a debate about the policies of the Taliban regime in Afghanistan: Were the Taliban's policies mandated by the Qur'an, permitted as one valid interpretation of the Qur'an but not required, or did they violate the letter or the spirit of the Qur'an? In order to make sure, as best I could, that the students took the Qur'an seriously, rather than dismissing the issue of what the Qur'an said and just giving their own opinions, I included a role-playing element: students were to write the essay as Muslim editors of a Middle Eastern newspaper; for them and for their readers, their editorial would be valid only if it effectively engaged in interpretation of the Qur'an.

At the beginning of September 2001, it was not to be expected that American college freshmen knew anything about the Taliban regime, so students were referred to an Internet site put out by an Afghan women's association that described the restrictions the Taliban regime imposed on women. Later that fall, of course, the regime became the focus of the news. As America prepared for war, the State Department posted on the Web a

White Paper on the plight of Afghan women. Before we reached the origins of Islam in class, Islam, its teachings, the Taliban regime, and their policies on women had all become front-page news throughout America and much of the world. Students debated vigorously, they used the Qur'an as evidence for their positions, they generally used Ahmed appropriately, and they had a lot of fun. Students felt empowered by their (relatively) deep understanding of public issues. Some students also noted in their on-line discussion the interesting fact that although the Taliban had been in power for years, it was only when America was gearing up for war with Afghanistan that the plight of Afghan women inspired public outrage on the part of the American government.

Growing Pains

Debates and the writing assignments that follow, by asking students to perform authentic historical tasks, expose weaknesses that remain hidden if students only repeat what they have heard in a lecture or answer factual questions. Bringing these weaknesses to the surface is therefore a good thing, making it possible to address these deficiencies and in the long term overcome them.

In the debates, as also in other contexts, one of the hardest things for students to do is to learn to engage in explicit commentary on what they are doing. I see this in several different areas: When evidence is contradictory, they tend to accept one view and ignore rather than rebut the other. An example is in the use of the Qur'an in the debate described above. A key verse is translated in two different ways that dramatically change the meaning and in turn powerfully affect the overall position of women in Islam. One translation says that the husband of a disobedient woman who has tried to change her conduct by admonition and by refusing to sleep with her may beat her. The other translation of the same verse says that women must be obedient to Allah, and that a woman who is unwilling to sleep with her husband must be left alone in the sleeping quarters, and he should only go in to her when she is willing. So one translation enjoins obedience to husbands for women as a religious duty and sanctions a husband beating a stubbornly disobedient wife. The other commands women to be obedient to God and prohibits what today we would call spousal rape. The translator of the second version explains in a footnote that the key issue is a term that can mean "beat" or can mean "have intercourse"; he says it cannot mean "beat" in this context because Muhammad is known in authentic hadiths to have said that one must not beat one's wife, and in another well-attested tradition the Prophet says one must not beat women at all. Although this issue was discussed in class, no students in their papers addressed the fact that there were two alternative versions of this text or discussed why they chose one interpretation over another.

I suspect that one reason students do not engage in this kind of commentary is that many students have been told in high school that they should never use "I" or "you" in a formal paper. Of course this often leads to ponderous writing and tortured passive-voice constructions. More seriously, it also probably contributes to the idea that formal writing is impersonal, presenting "just the facts," and refers neither to the author nor to the reader. Although the goal is laudable, it is a barrier to the development of an effective argumentative style. We should make clear that far from being weakened by argument on why translation A is more likely to represent what was said than translation B, academic writing is strengthened by this kind of commentary.

Another major weakness of student writing is the reluctance to engage contrary evidence (Graff, 2003). There is a strong tendency to ignore it, perhaps because students do not recognize the contradiction, perhaps in the hope no one else will realize that it is there. My expectation was that the debates would make that head-in-the-sand strategy impossible: someone would be bound to bring up inconvenient evidence, and students would then have to deal with it during the debate, and this would carry over to their essays. This proved unduly optimistic on my part.

When the students almost all failed to address contrary positions in their papers, in spite of having confronted them in class and in spite of having a written rubric that indicated this was essential to an A paper, I added a new step for the first essay, a debate on Athenian democracy. In addition to the assignment sheet, students were also given the self-check sheet (see Exhibit 3.1).

Students were instructed to bring their drafts to the class session before the essays were due. They used green pens I distributed to mark up their drafts, labeling the thesis, their use of textual evidence, their confrontation of counterarguments, and so on. If they discovered their essays lacked any of these components, they were encouraged to write in either specific information or a note such as "check Thucydides on this." They were instructed to revise their papers and turn in both the marked-up draft and the final draft. To help them make the transition to being better editors of their own work, at the next debate I had them draft their own self-check sheets in class using the writing assignment, and I then posted a final version on Blackboard, combining the strongest points raised in class. I also suggested that as they wrote papers in other classes, it would be useful for them to use the assignment to make up their own self-check sheets and review their drafts to make sure they had fulfilled all the requirements before turning in their final papers.

This process helped; a majority of the essays were improved by the self-check list, and none were actually made worse. Students' notes to themselves included reminders like "add more primary sources," "check Critias," "counter-arg here!" Sometimes the in-class recognition that changes were needed did not actually lead to making changes in the final draft. There were also instances where the self-check revealed misunderstanding on the part of the student, so that he or she thought a criterion had been met when

Exhibit 3.1. Writing Assignment Self-Check Sheet

Your assignment asks you to make an argument on the assigned topic and says that an excellent paper will do the following:
• Include a clear thesis
• Offer specific evidence from both primary and secondary texts to support your thesis
• Make clear how that evidence supports your position
• Address and rebut counterarguments

Using the green pen provided, mark your draft essay as follows:
• If your thesis makes a specific claim, place a check mark here: _____ .
• Underline your thesis with a straight line.
• Circle instances in which you provide specific evidence from the texts to support your argument.
• Add up the number of times you use evidence from primary sources and write that number here: _____ .
• Add up the number of references to the scholarly work (whether to agree with or disagree with it) and enter the number here: _____ .
• Use a wavy line to underline specific statements that show how a piece of evidence supports your argument.
• Put brackets [   ] around passages where you address and rebut counterarguments.
• If any element is weak or lacking, use the green pen to insert a reference or phrase to remind yourself what you need to revise at home. Mark these revisions with a star.

Your paper should now be covered with green—symbol of life, of growth, of hope!

At home, revise: strengthen, clarify, add evidence, make explicit connections between your evidence and your thesis, confront alternative arguments, polish your writing, double-check grammar, spelling, and usage.

Turn in the marked-up draft, this sheet, and your final revised essay on the due date for this assignment.

---

it had not. This allowed me to clear up misunderstandings I would not have known existed if I had not seen on their self-check sheets and marked-up drafts their own view of what they had done.

Yet another weakness is that even when students adduce a piece of evidence to support their position, they very rarely state explicitly how this evidence is to be read or the point it supports. It is as if they thrust their argument and the evidence before reader, side by side, and to them the connection is obvious and does not need to be made explicit. The self-check sheet asked them to note whether they had made clear the links between the evidence they offered and the point they were trying to prove. Some of the check sheets included notes like "Add sentence here," or "Explain: So what?" As with the other material, they were not always successful in translating this into effective argumentation, but the realization that such connections were needed was a step forward in itself.

Results

There is no doubt that the debates help toward the goal of engagement. The vast majority of students state in anonymous end-of-term surveys that for the second half of the world history sequence, they would prefer a debate class. When I was teaching two sections, one with debates and another discussing the same materials, but without debates, the non-debate class referred to the other as the "fun class." They finally pressured me into allowing at least one informal debate in their class as well. Even those (10 percent or fewer) who would have preferred a class without debates usually say that they dislike debates because they hate to speak out in class or they hate the pressure they feel to talk. Only a few students over several years have said that they think the debates are a waste of time. As well as student preference, it is worth noting that more than 90 percent of the class typically participates in the debates, compared to much lower rates of class participation in less-structured discussions.

The creation of the self-check sheet, as opposed to my commenting on drafts, was originally driven by time constraints. Yet this is an instance in which one can make a virtue of necessity: I think students learned more from checking their own work and trying to grapple with what the assignment really asked of them and how well they had fulfilled it. And the comparison of what they thought they had done with what they actually had achieved made clear to me certain misunderstandings that I could then try to forestall before later debates and in teaching the course in the future.

The tie-in to current events has also been a success, furthering both the disciplinary goal of encouraging students to see contemporary events in historical context and the citizenship goal. Obviously, current events have provided a great deal of material related to the debate on Islam, but we do not depend on a national tragedy to make history relevant and interesting. Students have gone beyond Afghanistan and Iraq in their posting of current events. To my delight, in addition to discussions of the veil as something imposed upon women, students have addressed situations in which a majority has refused to allow women to observe the veil, such as the recent French prohibition of expressions of religious identity in public schools, including a ban on wearing head scarves, or the refusal of the Turkish parliament to allow a female elected representative to take her seat when she refused to abandon her head scarf. A couple of students have even applied the idea of the tyranny of the majority, a concept discussed in relation to Athenian democracy, to this kind of imposition of a secular orthodoxy upon a minority.

While I have no longitudinal data to prove it, it is possible that the debates will address the well-attested problems that exist in the transfer of learning outside the classroom. The combination of active student participation in learning in the debates with explicit exploration of the links to current events outside the classroom may help these students to avoid those pitfalls.

Students also indicate in the anonymous surveys that they feel they have changed. Some describe this in purely academic terms, stating, for example, that they have learned the material better for having to defend it. Others say they have learned to think on their feet or to speak before a group. Occasionally a debate will have even more personal meaning for a student. One Muslim student, who dressed modestly but did not cover her hair, told me that reading the primary sources and scholarship on Islam had given her arguments to use against those who pressured her to wear a head scarf: she felt she could defend the legitimacy of her choice in a way she had not been able to do before.

In all of these areas, therefore, the project has been to some degree a success. But this is a limited and fragile beginning.

In a research project that grew out of the development of the series of debates, I also analyzed essay exams to see whether experience of debates stimulated more sophisticated intellectual achievement even in treatment of issues that were not part of the debates. Ideally, the experience in the debates should promote this kind of thinking applied to other issues as well. Unfortunately, the study did not demonstrate that kind of broader transformation. I imagine that there are several reasons for this. For example, students could not necessarily change in quantifiable ways after a single semester, or the skills of debate don't generalize to other forms of argumentation. This kind of more generalized sophistication would probably appear, if at all, much further along in the student's intellectual development. Partly, it may take many experiences over many domains before the habits of mind become generalized. In accordance with the concept of the paradigm shift discussed in this volume by Ned Laff, preconceptions do not fall before the first piece of contrary evidence; it is only over time and as many contradictions accumulate that the existing paradigm finally crumbles.

The fragility of student development is a strong argument for intentionality in setting goals and in designing assignments and other activities to further those goals. Certainly, students who have participated in debates do begin to think more critically about history, and the surveys and students' spontaneous comments suggest that they also begin to apply their historical knowledge in their own real-life situations. This is only the first step in a lifelong journey.

References

Ahmed, Leila. *Women and Gender in Islam: The Historical Roots of a Modern Debate.* New Haven: Yale University Press, 1992.

Colby, A., Ehrlich, T., Beaumont, E., and Stephens, J. *Educating Citizens: Preparing America's Undergraduates for Lives of Moral and Civic Responsibility.* San Francisco: Jossey-Bass, 2003.

Graff, G. *Clueless in Academe: How Schooling Obscures the Life of the Mind.* New Haven: Yale University Press, 2003.

Mill, J. S. *On Liberty and Utilitarianism*. New York: Bantam Classics, 1993. (Originally published 1859.)

National Research Council. *How People Learn: Brain, Mind, Experience, and School*. Washington, D.C.: National Academy Press, 1999.

Perry, W. G., Jr. *Forms of Intellectual and Ethical Development in the College Years: A Scheme*. Austin, Tex.: Holt, Rinehart, and Winston, 1970.

Stewart, J. *Crossfire* [television program], CNN, October 15, 2004.

Walvoord, B. E., and Breihan, J. E. "Arguing and Debating: Breihan's History Course." In E. P. Walvoord and L. P. McCarthy (eds.), *Thinking and Writing in College: A Naturalistic Study of Students in Four Disciplines*. Urbana: National Council of Teachers of English, 1990.

Wineburg, S. *Historical Thinking and Other Unnatural Acts: Charting the Future of Teaching the Past*. Philadelphia: Temple University Press, 2001.

Woodruff, P. *First Democracy: The Challenge of an Ancient Idea*. Oxford: Oxford University Press, 2004.

ANNE OSBORNE *is professor of history and chair of the History Department at Rider University.*

4

General-education science courses should provide
students with a foundation of knowledge about how the
natural world works, a clear understanding of the nature
of science and scientific inquiry, and an appreciation for
the relationship between science and society. This chapter
suggests a variety of approaches to engage students in
their own learning and, with appropriate reflection, help
them construct more scientific worldviews.

Reshaping Their Views: Science as Liberal Arts

Judith Bramble

> If we teach only the findings and products of science—no matter
> how useful and even inspiring they may be—without communi-
> cating its critical method, how can the average person possibly
> distinguish science from pseudoscience?
> —Carl Sagan, 1996, p. 21

I enjoy teaching general-education science because I like to see the light
bulbs go on. It is not that science majors do not have meaningful learning
moments as well, but most have mastered the art of learning science and
can comfortably package new information into an existing architecture of
knowledge. Then, too, we have four years with which to influence their
understanding of how the world works and how we know it. We have fewer
opportunities to help the non-science major and we are often hampered at
the start with student science deficiencies, misconceptions, and fears.

One of my goals is that students appreciate the value of learning science, and of this they usually report positive gains. Lately, though, I have
been wondering if I have really changed the way they look at science and
the world around them. Last year, as part of a collegewide assessment of
critical thinking, I had students critique an unsupported scientific claim and
an uncontrolled scientific experiment at the start and end of a course on scientific inquiry. For the most part, their answers were as uncritical and unso-
phisticated at the end of the course as at the start. Was I expecting too much
in thinking that a course on how science works would make a difference?

NEW DIRECTIONS FOR TEACHING AND LEARNING, no. 103, Fall 2005 © Wiley Periodicals, Inc.

Scientific literacy is about developing in our students the knowledge and habits of mind to be able to evaluate evidence and express well-informed and reasoned opinions on scientific issues of importance in today's society (American Association for the Advancement of Science (AAAS), 1990; National Research Council, 1996). Most Americans have limited scientific knowledge and a poor understanding of how science works (National Science Board (NSB), 2004). In the general public, belief in pseudoscientific phenomena such as extrasensory perception and astrology is widespread, and there is evidence it has increased over the past decade (NSB, 2004).

Content-rich courses for science majors often overwhelm underprepared non-majors who fail to make meaningful connections between the material and their lives. Thematic, interdisciplinary courses that place science in the context of students' lives help them make these connections and so, we hope, move them toward scientific literacy. But without an understanding of how we know what we know, what the strengths and limits of scientific inquiry are, and how to evaluate evidence critically, students build knowledge by adding interesting and meaningful information into a worldview that is still full of misunderstandings about the natural world around them. I recently had non-major students read a nicely designed research article testing the hypothesis that college students gain fifteen pounds during their freshman year (Graham and Jones, 2002). My students were able to read and correctly interpret the data, which showed an overall loss of weight for the small cohort followed in the study. When I asked my students if they thought the study failed to support the hypothesis, they all agreed, but then added that they still believed in the "Freshman 15" phenomenon because they had seen it for themselves.

We all seek patterns of order and meaning in the world around us. We develop our worldviews from our observations, both direct and indirect. When our observations do not mesh with our explanations, we can either ignore the observations or reexamine the explanations as we continue to build our worldviews. A scientific worldview incorporates skepticism, creativity, and analysis in pursuing puzzling observations, and although that worldview doesn't guarantee correct interpretations, we believe that it provides us with the best way of learning about the natural world. In fact, the strongest scientific studies attempt to disprove our understandings, accepting that if they stand up to that level of scrutiny, they are more likely to be correct.

Scientists are motivated to understand how the world works. Approaches that lead them astray are ultimately counterproductive. An unscientific approach, in contrast, takes comfort in uncritically making new observations fit into favored explanations. I have a friend who believes that a certain over-the-counter medication, if taken at the first sign of cold symptoms, will prevent the development of the cold. If it does, his belief is reinforced. If it does not, he explains that he did not take it early enough. Every observation supports and strengthens his worldview, though it is most likely incorrect.

The worldviews that students bring into class are not necessarily challenged by even the most engaging science content. The course's factual information is neatly stored (or not) with the rest of the student's growing understanding of the way the world works. Students' notions need to be challenged in a way that gets them uncomfortable with the knowledge and allows them to reshape their understandings of the world. Student understandings about the nature of science and scientific inquiry need to make them more critical purveyors of new information and more appreciative of the strengths and limits of science in society. Four kinds of experiences, with appropriate reflection, should help accomplish these goals:

- Student-centered, open-ended scientific investigations
- Experience with the primary scientific literature
- Familiarity with the people who do science, both good and bad, in historic and recent times
- Opportunities to work on meaningful, ill-structured problems

Student-Centered, Open-Ended Scientific Investigations

The college science laboratory is traditionally a place for students to gain first-hand experience with the material described in lecture, to practice using the tools of science, and to go through the steps of a scientific investigation. Many college labs are written in a cookbook fashion, with a certain outcome used as a measure of successful completion of the lab assignment. Writing structured scientific lab reports is a skill that is mastered through feedback and repetition. Students quickly learn what is expected of them. They not only value expected results over the unexpected, but they become frustrated when the lab work doesn't progress as expected by the instructor. My colleagues sometimes complain that students do not read the lab instructions before coming to class and that students would get more out of lab if they did. While true, unless there are penalties for not doing so, there is not much incentive for the student. This is not "minds-on" work.

National reform efforts aimed at promoting scientific literacy argue for the importance of modeling the process of doing science through inquiry-focused science lab experiences (AAAS, 1990; National Research Council, 1996). The goal is not to make the student into a scientist, but by modeling the process, to create the experiences to ground an understanding of how science is done. In addition, if the student generates a question and the answer is not necessarily known, the motivation to answer the question drives the process. The focus, then, for both student and instructor, is in using good scientific reasoning and the appropriate use of scientific tools to answer the question. In addition, these experiences provide an opportunity for the development of scientific habits of mind, including creative expression, trust in observations, and the excitement of discovery.

The challenge at the college level is in designing authentic, student-centered research experiences using the equipment and time available. My experience using this approach with non-science majors is that the students do become engaged in the process and design reasonably good experiments given the time and resources available. However, I have found that the product of their investigation, usually a research report or poster presentation, to be a less than satisfying way to end this process. Student-generated questions are rarely answered in the time frame of the course, and the conclusions they reach often support the original hypothesis even when the data do not warrant it. The end of the investigation becomes focused on the final product, and the interest in answering the question as well as the lessons learned about the process of doing science become lost. The final product ends the student's scientific investigation, but should not end the learning experience. Students need to critique each other's experimental design, data analysis, assumptions, and conclusions and be given the opportunity to respond to such critiques in a continuous dialogue so they can come to terms with what they discovered and revisit the quality of their evidence and the role of scientific inquiry in answering their questions of how the world works.

Recent studies in science education have shown that simply engaging in the practice of scientific inquiry may not be sufficient to change the learner's understandings about the nature of science; experience doing science grounded in active reflection of the learning process may be needed to effect change (Adb-El-Khalik and Lederman, 2000; Schwartz, Lederman, and Crawford, 2004 and references therein). In fact, one of the most intriguing aspects of these studies is the suggestion that scientists themselves may not be able to articulate reasonably contemporary views on the nature of science (Schwartz, Lederman, and Crawford, 2004). That is, successfully performing a scientific investigation may not depend on the scientist actively reflecting on the philosophical underpinnings of his or her work. However, science teachers, including university faculty, must have an explicit understanding of the nature of science, "the meaning of science, assumptions, values, conceptual inventions, method, consensus making and characteristics of the knowledge produced" (Schwartz, Lederman, and Crawford, 2004, p. 612) if that is a goal of their instruction and if they are to develop these understandings in their students.

Experience with the Primary Scientific Literature

Doing science and then reflecting on the learning process will move students toward scientific literacy. The reality, however, is that lab investigations are finite research experiences with limits to discovery imposed by the time and equipment constraints of a student course exercise. Students are motivated to solve an intriguing puzzle and generally enjoy the process, but they often do not see the relevance to their lives and to society. These experiences can be reinforced by having students read original research articles that show how knowledge is moved forward in meaningful ways through this process of discovery.

Until recently, I did not have non-science students read original scientific research articles. I thought that without sufficient content knowledge and vocabulary, let alone statistical knowledge, the students simply would not get anything out of it. Instead I provided copies of research articles for students to look over to reinforce their basic understanding of the scientific process and to use as models of scientific writing for their lab reports. I first had non-science majors actually read and analyze a research article in a course that focused on scientific inquiry. I chose a short, readable paper in a peer-reviewed journal that tested a hypothesis I thought would interest the students. As an assignment, I asked specific questions about the hypothesis being tested, the design of the experiment, evidence presented in support of the hypothesis, and the general organization of the paper. I asked about the strengths and limitations of the study and finally, if they agreed with the conclusions of the study. The students were quite capable of reading and analyzing the paper but had trouble identifying its strengths and limitations. This was tied to their tendency to accept or reject the conclusions of the article based on their personal experience, not on the quality of the evidence. I realized that students do not understand variation and the nature of scientific data.

In *Benchmarks for Science Literacy* (AAAS, 1993), the authors say that in early elementary school, students need to understand that when they do an experiment in the same way, they will get the same results. By the end of elementary school, they need to know that this is not always the case. By the end of middle school, students should know that the "scientific challenge is to judge whether the differences are trivial or significant" and that it usually requires additional studies to decide (p. 7). In Graham and Jones's Freshman 15 study I mentioned earlier, although the average subject lost weight, some freshmen lost up to fifteen pounds and some gained up to fifteen pounds. My non-science students did not know how to handle this variation. They supported their own impressions that the phenomenon was true by pointing out that some students in the study did in fact gain fifteen pounds. It took quite a bit of prodding for them to acknowledge that the average student in this study did not gain weight and that the fact that there was variation was both interesting and important and could lead to a better understanding of the phenomenon and to the next set of questions to study. It was fine to still believe in the Freshman 15 phenomenon, but these new beliefs needed to incorporate the results of this study and be treated as testable, new hypotheses.

The analysis of published articles offers a good opportunity to reflect on how science works, including the role of anecdote and creativity in developing hypotheses, the importance of testing hypotheses and designing good experiments, the strengths and limits of experimentation, the importance of trust in evidence, and the setbacks to solving problems we can face when we accept hypotheses without testing them. It also permits a better understanding of the process and power of peer review in science and provides another segue to a discussion of science as a social process.

A corollary to providing research articles to students is encouraging them to use the primary literature to help answer questions that matter to them. This is not an easy task for students, who frequently do not know how to use their libraries' resources to find relevant scientific research studies and then have trouble wading through the jargon and sophisticated methodological and statistical procedures. At some point in their lives, though, when they need answers to health or other science-related questions that truly matter to them, we would like our former students to value scientific evidence over anecdote and pseudoscientific claims. They need to know how to search for answers to their questions directly or indirectly from the scientific literature.

Familiarity with the People and Stories of Science

Scientific discoveries occur within the context of the prevailing scientific worldview and social setting. What we know about the natural world and how we study it have changed dramatically over time, even the recent past. Our students come to us not understanding that factual knowledge of the world accumulates even as our explanations to account for it change. Students have difficulty understanding why scientists do not agree with each other and how prevailing scientific wisdom, for example on health recommendations or environmental issues, can change dramatically based on new evidence or new ways of looking at old evidence. Some students distrust science because they see scientific explanations as changeable and unreliable. Having students examine historical accounts of how we know what we know gives them an appreciation that scientific knowledge is provisional and builds on or replaces (and so, still builds on) progress made in the past. The goal is to understand that current scientific explanations, while they may be revised in the future, are still the best explanations we have for how the natural world works.

Scientists perform science and scientists make mistakes. Sigma Xi's handbook, *Honor in Science* (1986), asks whether fraud and abuse are rare in science or whether the spectacular cases we see from time to time reflect just the tip of an iceberg. The system of peer review and the process of building on prior scientific discovery should expose bad science. A hallmark of pseudoscience is that it usually does not go through normal science channels, but is often presented directly to the public. Students enjoy learning about poorly designed experiments and about deliberate fraud and other abuses of science. Students need exposure to bad science, both deliberate and unintentional, to understand how easily we are fooled by what seems to be scientific information or experimentation. Students should be trained to ask, "How was that claim tested" each time they are exposed to new public announcements of scientific progress.

Opportunities to Work with Ill-Structured Problems

As we move our students toward better understandings of how science works, we need to provide opportunities for them to put their new scientific knowledge and understandings to work in an attempt to solve problems that are meaningful to them and important to society. We need to provide students with the opportunity to work with messy, ill-structured problems that are informed by, but not necessarily solved by, scientific information. Case studies provide an opportunity for students to ground scientific knowledge and develop scientific habits of mind, including critical thinking, problem solving, skepticism, and flexibility (Herreid, 2004; see also the National Center for Case Study Teaching in Science online at http://ublib.buffalo.edu/libraries/projects/cases/case.html). The Science Education for New Civic Engagements and Responsibilities project (SENCER) provides models and workshops for college educators as well as a national assessment project to see if the use of complex, unsolved public-science issues develops students' science skills, interests, and civic engagement (Seymour, 2002). Both the National Center for Case Study Teaching in Science and SENCER help faculty develop their own case study modules; SENCER also offers support for using their modules in large lecture classes.

Local issues can provide opportunities for authentic research on messy real-world problems. I have had several classes of non-science students assess local biodiversity and use historical records to describe the very clear changes in species composition in our natural lands over the past thirty to two hundred years. The content of the course provides information about the general causes of species loss, but the clear explanations in the book become difficult to apply to the changes occurring locally. When students do field and library research and seek out experts within the community, they find that there are several different explanations offered, in many cases depending on the species, biological community, or expert consulted. Restoration ecology is a dynamic field in which experts often disagree about both methods and goals. In every class I have engaged in clearing nonnative plant species, there are always a few students who insist that the plants we are about to cut down have value and deserve to remain. These feelings are projections of one of many possible environmental values that students have likely never articulated. By exploring personal values, ecological knowledge, and environmental goals, students with different personal beliefs can come up with a consensus plan for restoration that respects and addresses competing value systems.

There are no clear answers to the problems of many of our pressing social issues that involve the application of scientific knowledge. As we use science to help us understand the consequences of our actions, we can better decide how we want to act. In the above example, students are reminded to ask, "How do you know" and "How could we test that" when they offer explanations for the changes they observe, and "What are the potential consequences of our actions" when they suggest changes in land-management

practices. The goal is to show students how important it is to have good scientific knowledge to make informed decisions, and how, ultimately, we may
have to choose among competing social needs with consequences to each
of our choices.

Science as Liberal Arts

What, then, do we want our students to know and be able to do as a result
of their general-education science experience? We want them to know more
science content—to know more about how the world works. We want them
to have an intuitive understanding of how science works and the nature
of science, and we want them to value and respect the evidence generated
by scientific investigations. We want them to understand how science contributes to our ability to solve pressing social problems, and we want them
both to trust in the process of peer review in science and to be critical of
unsubstantiated claims.

Science literacy, then, is more than transmitting essential understandings about how the world works. In fact, we have to decide in what
content to ground these other understandings because there is far too
much science content knowledge to fit into the undergraduate experience
even for the science major. We should be deliberate in our choice of science content and select content that both provides essential background
for pressing issues in today's world and also affords the opportunity to
learn how we know what we know about science. We want to create those
"aha" moments that show that our students connect with the knowledge,
but that also show that they understand that science is a powerful way of
making sense out of the natural world.

We do not do this by watering down science major courses. I have too
often heard science faculty claim that general-education science courses
are "baby science," as if factual knowledge is the prize. We do have an obli-
gation to our science majors to give them sufficient depth of science content knowledge and experience with the tools of scientific inquiry to
prepare them successfully for careers in science. Beyond that, the goals
should be similar for both groups of students. We have less opportunity to
address these goals with our non-science majors, so we have to be intentional in our planning to meet them. One might argue that we should be
more deliberate in our work with our science majors as well. Johnson and
Pigliucci (2004) administered a survey to biology students in sophomore-
level science courses and to business students in sophomore-level philosophy courses. The questions addressed factual science content, science
process understandings, and pseudoscientific beliefs. The results showed
that, while science students knew significantly more science content, they
showed equally poor understandings of how science works and equally
unskeptical responses to pseudoscientific beliefs. Perhaps these science
students will develop better understandings of the nature of science over

their undergraduate career. It is likely that we need to build in explicit reflection about the nature of science and scientific inquiry with our science majors as well.

We might consider expanding the use of undergraduate science students in service learning as peer tutors and interpreters of science for non-science majors. The key is to ensure that the science students understand not only the content material, but also the goals of science education and the nature of science and scientific inquiry. The benefits would be to both sets of students. The science education literature is expansive on the attributes that characterize the nature of science and these understandings are at the heart of decades of reform efforts in pre-college science education (see Lederman, 1992). Most science faculty have no contact with this literature, and no matter what instructional strategies we adopt in our courses, it's hard to imagine how we will change student understandings about the nature of science until we make these understandings an explicit priority in our undergraduate science instruction.

The good news is that the general public does support science and recognize its value even if they don't understand it (NSB, 2004). However, as journalist Boyce Rensberger points out, "without a grasp of scientific ways of thinking, the average person cannot tell the difference between science based on real data and something that resembles science . . . but is based on uncontrolled experiments, anecdotal evidence, and passionate assertions. They like it all" (Rensberger, 2000). The role of science education is to fill in the gap. Universities have a triple role to play here. We influence the development of scientists, future educators, and, through our students' general education, a large proportion of the general public. The prize in science education is in a deeper understanding of how we know what we know in science—in understanding about the nature of science and scientific inquiry. Disciplinary content grounds these understandings. Interdisciplinary knowledge and methodology prepare our students to contribute to the solution of problems that society faces.

Our general-education science program can meet these goals by providing opportunities for students to develop more scientific ways of thinking. We can encourage students to generate their own questions and help them design experiments to answer them. Students can read, evaluate, and discuss scientific research articles and connect them to problems that society is grappling with today. Students can see how society has influenced the course of science and how scientific discoveries have affected society. We can give students concrete examples of science done poorly (or not at all, though in the name of science) and the opportunity to use their knowledge to solve messy but meaningful problems. We can do all of this in a way that challenges students to confront their worldviews and actively reflect on their learning. We can plan our general-education program to create these experiences and move our students toward science literacy if we ourselves keep our eyes on the prize.

References

Adb-El-Khalik, F., and Lederman, N. G. "Improving Science Teachers' Conceptions of Nature of Science: A Critical Review of the Literature." *International Journal of Science Education,* 2000, 22(7), 665–702.

American Association for the Advancement of Science (AAAS). *Science for All Americans.* New York: Oxford University Press, 1990.

American Association for the Advancement of Science. *Benchmarks for Science Literacy: A Project 2061 Report.* New York: Oxford University Press, 1993.

Graham, M., and Jones, A. L. "Freshman 15: Valid Theory or Harmful Myth?" *Journal of American College Health,* 2002, 50(4), 171–174.

Herreid, C. F. "Can Case Studies Be Used to Teach Critical Thinking?" *Journal of College Science Teaching,* 2004, 33(6), 12–14.

Johnson, M., and Pigliucci, M. "Is Knowledge of Science Associated with Higher Skepticism of Pseudoscientific Claims?" *American Biology Teacher,* 2004, 66(8), 536–546.

Lederman, N. G. "Students' and Teachers' Conceptions of the Nature of Science: A Review of the Research." *Journal of Research in Science Teaching,* 1992, 29, 331–359.

National Research Council. *National Science Education Standards.* Washington, D.C.: National Academy Press, 1996.

National Science Board (NSB). *Science and Engineering Indicators—2004.* Washington, D.C.: U.S. Government Printing Office, 2004.

Rensberger, B. "The Nature of Evidence." *Science,* 2000, 289(5476), 61.

Sagan, C. *The Demon-Haunted World: Science as a Candle in the Dark.* New York: Random House, 1996.

Schwartz, R. S., Lederman, N. G., and Crawford, B. A. "Developing Views of Nature of Science in an Authentic Context: An Explicit Approach to Bridging the Gap Between Nature of Science and Scientific Inquiry." *Science Education,* 2004, 88(4), 610–646.

Seymour, E. "Tracking the Processes of Change in U.S. Undergraduate Education in Science, Mathematics, Engineering, and Technology." *Science Education,* 2002, 86(1), 79–106.

Sigma Xi. *Honor in Science.* Research Triangle Park, N.C.: Sigma Xi, the Scientific Research Society, 1986.

JUDITH BRAMBLE is associate professor in the Environmental Science Program at DePaul University.

5

Service-learning courses can be powerful instruments for cognitive, affective, and moral transformation. This chapter examines the strengths and weaknesses of service-learning as an agent for cognitive, moral, and interpersonal development and its ability to promote civic or social engagement.

Pedagogy and Practice: Service-Learning and Students' Moral Development

Charles R. Strain

> A monk asked Dong-shan: "Is there a practice for people to follow?" Dong-shan answered: "When you become a real person, there is such a practice."
>
> —Gary Snyder, 1990, p. 185

There is a heady ferment in the scholarship on the pedagogy of service-learning. Researchers agree that service-learning courses can be powerful instruments for cognitive, affective, and moral transformation (Eyler and Giles, 1999). We are beginning to define best practices in the pedagogy of service-learning, most particularly around the role of reflective exercises in achieving the interlocking goals of such courses. Developmental theorists like Anne Colby argue that "Experiential learning, including service-learning, centrally acknowledges the context specificity of learning, providing educational settings that are less artificial than the classroom and much closer to the contexts in which students will later perform. When these settings are explicitly civic, as they are in service-learning . . . , they provide stronger support for moral and civic development than most lectures or seminars can" (Colby, Ehrlich, Beaumont, and Stephens, 2003, p. 139).

Note: I am grateful to all of the students in experiential and service-learning classes that I have taught, but here especially to Andrea Barrera, Christina Ferantelli, Cara Joyce, Joshua McCarty, and Ben Nowicki for their ideas and written reflections in this article. I am also grateful to Sister Jane Gerard, C.S.J. for her assistance in researching this article and preparing the manuscript.

Careful studies are beginning to show, on the one hand, how service-learning works, and when, on the other hand, it can reinforce frozen attitudes and negative stereotypes (Eyler and Giles, 1999). The key, all agree, is using oral and written reflective exercises to connect cognitive inquiry with the experience of service in order to propel a lasting transformation on multiple levels. Defining reflection as the "intentional consideration of an experience in light of particular learning objectives," Julie Hatcher and associates (Hatcher, Bringle, and Muthiah, 2004, p. 38) weigh the empirical evidence for what kinds of reflective exercises work. "Specifically, reflection that is structured, regular and clarifies values *independently*," they conclude, "contributed to the quality of the educational experience for students" (Hatcher, Bringle, and Muthiah, p. 42; emphasis in original).

All well and good. But in the different areas that service-learning courses are shown to be effective, what are the "particular learning objectives" to be sought? Toward what ends should the reflective exercises be directed? This becomes an especially tricky set of questions if we ask them with regard to students' moral development. In what follows I will link an analysis of the different components of moral development and the kind of evolution that each requires with examples of oral and written exercises that serve to catalyze these processes in service-learning classes. I will also draw on the writings and reflections of students in recent service-learning classes to illustrate each component.

Moral Development: The State of the Art

In their recent massive update to their equally massive review of the research literature on how college affects students, Ernest Pascarella and Patrick Terenzini (2005) reaffirm their 1991 conclusion that "college is linked with statistical increases in the use of principled moral reasoning to judge moral issues. . . . However, the exact magnitude of the gain may not be as important as the movement from conventional to postconventional or principled judgment during college, which in itself is an important event in moral development (pp. 345–346). For many of those who seek to promote civic engagement, moral development is synonymous with this access to a "post-conventional" level of moral judgment that emphasizes the autonomous grasp of putatively universal moral principles focused on rights and justice. This understanding of moral development is rooted in the theory and pioneering work of Lawrence Kohlberg (1971, 1981, 1984). Kohlberg's theory posited six stages of moral development that were irreversible, structural reorganizations of thinking about moral issues. Anne Colby states it this way: "As individuals move through the successive stages, their moral judgment moves from simple conceptions of morality grounded in unilateral authority and individual reciprocity to judgments grounded in shared social norms to an appreciation of a more complex social system to a perspective that is capable of evaluating the existing social system in relation to more fundamental principles of justice" (Colby, Ehrlich, Beaumont, and Stephens, 2003, pp. 103–104).

For obvious reasons Kohlberg's emphasis on the cognitive component in moral development has been very attractive to educators. As Colby puts it, it is "impossible to divide moral and civic development sharply from intellectual or academic development because much of moral and civic development *is* intellectual" (Colby, Ehrlich, Beaumont, and Stephens, 2003, p. 105; emphasis in the original). However, many scholars over the past quarter of a century have challenged not so much the substance of Kohlberg's theory but its claims to uncover universal, cognitive-moral structures. Beginning with Carol Gilligan's well-known charge of gender bias and her juxtaposition of an "ethic of care" to Kohlberg's "abstract" ethic of procedural justice, scholars have questioned the cross-cultural validity and the concept of irreversible stages that are part and parcel of Kohlberg's theory (Gilligan, 1982). As we will see shortly, the most important qualifications of Kohlberg's theory are those that point out what Kohlberg himself acknowledged, namely, that reasoning toward moral judgment is only one component of moral development (Rest, Narváez, Bebeau, and Thoma, 1999).

From Charity to Justice

Before we pick up on this qualification, however, it is important to assess how service-learning courses have traditionally handled the issue of moral development at the course level. In workshop after workshop, as well as in much of the literature, I have heard faculty describe their learning goal relative to moral development as a shift in students' consciousness from charity to social justice. Narratives such as that of teaching people to fish (or even assisting people in creating fish farms) versus providing them with fish— supplement Kohlberg in suggesting a unilinear evolution. Even Eyler and Giles (1999) frequently see the transformational power of service-learning in terms of a transition from "patronizing" charity to "a greater sense of the importance of political action to obtain social justice" (pp. 47, 135).

In the service-learning courses that I teach I, too, am concerned that students think systemically about the causes of injustice and that they frame their moral judgments based on such an analysis. Yet my students tell me repeatedly that it is the relationships that they enter into with inspiring community leaders, with immigrants struggling to learn English, with inner-city kids in after-school programs, and even long-distance relationships with embattled human rights workers in Latin America that are morally transformative. In a recent final reflection paper for an experiential study abroad and service-learning course, Andrea Barrera put it this way:

> [The] power of relationships is often overlooked in daily activity, even in historic events. In order to accomplish a large change or transformation, there needs to be this stability of relationships. A voice is only as strong as

the relationships developed in order for it to be heard. A person can kick, scream, and march all around, but it is not until they actually work to formulate the relationships and build their credibility amongst a network, that people will be more likely to listen and want to help bring about change. Therefore, empowering others is essentially empowering the relationship. . . . I know what gets me going, and it is the people themselves, not the policy that we learned. I would rather get to know the people on the interpersonal level, and then, from there, make decisions on how to help. On the other hand there are people out there who do enjoy the policies and creating rules and regulations to help the people. By working together, people can effectively be heard, and change can occur.

Andrea could be seen as exemplifying Carol Gilligan's "ethic of care" and validating her argument. However, I want to suggest that what is truly illuminating in Andrea's reflection is her level of self-awareness ("I know what gets me going") and her realization that it takes networking among people who bring to bear a variety of cognitive skills, moral frameworks, and action orientations to create social change. Keith Morton's experience with his students has also led him to reject any dichotomy of charity and justice as a way of construing the moral field that is opened up by service-learning experiences. Learning from students like Andrea, Morton (2002) suggests that we look at different types of service (charity, community-empowering projects, and justice-oriented change processes) as representing different worldviews, each of which can lead to a moral development if plumbed in depth and with "integrity and courage" (p. 46).

The Components of a Moral Life

This brings us back to Kohlberg's stages. In my judgment, the most important evolution in post-Kohlbergian research focuses on the exploration of components of a moral life other than moral reasoning and judgment. Immediately, however, we run into the problem of a number of different ways of slicing the moral cake. While categories, terminology, and emphases differ, the cake looks pretty much the same. So, I will use the four-component model developed by James Rest and his associates. Keep in mind that each component of the moral life represents a process that must be undergone if moral development is to occur.

1. Moral *sensitivity* (. . . being aware that there is a moral problem when it exists)
2. Moral *judgment* (judging which action would be most justifiable in a moral sense . . .)
3. Moral *motivation* (the degree of commitment to taking the moral course of action . . .)

4. Moral *character* (persisting in a moral task . . .) [Rest, Narváez, Bebeau, and Thoma, 1999, p. 101; see also pp. 100–103 and Narváez and Rest, 1995]

As soon as we think of each of these components as a process, our view of moral development changes. Perhaps we should think of moral development as growing complexity and integration along multiple vectors rather than as a unilinear movement through fixed stages.

Moral Sensitivity. In one of my recent service-learning classes, Josh McCarty chose to volunteer at the Chicago Religious Leadership Network (CRLN), an organization that supports human rights workers and advocates for social justice in Latin America. CRLN has devised an ingenious way of putting college students to work. It gives them case files of imprisoned or endangered human rights workers, asks them to research the case, and then write a letter in support of this actual person to heads of government, CEOs of multinational corporations, and others who have the power to alter the situation. DePaul students sign their own name to the letter with the title "Human Rights Assistant" underneath. At the first class session, Josh allowed that the proximity of CRLN's office to his apartment and the opportunity to improve his writing skills were his primary motivations in his choice of a service placement. To be sure, this was not atypical of our pragmatic students and, in fact, I always stress that service-learning can be an important means to enhance career skills.

At our second class session, Josh came back with a different story. It was as if a light bulb in a dark room had been switched on. As he studied his first case file, he became aware that an actual human person's life hung in the balance. This was not an opportunity to pursue his self-interest, but rather the person herself morally obligated Josh to write the best letter that he could whether or not it would alter the situation. Josh exhibited not only a keen moral sensitivity but combined it with a sense of moral seriousness. He moved from a utilitarian calculation to an internalization of his designated role as human rights advocate. In my experience, the situations themselves that we place students in when we teach service-learning classes have the power to evoke moral sensitivity and seriousness far better than concocting moral dilemmas or than my raising questions based on even the best readings.

Not always, however. In another service-learning class a premed student assigned to work as a teacher's aide in an after-school program in an inner-city elementary school exploded in disgust after her first experience with her public school teacher: "She doesn't even know what a femur is." (You can imagine my instant panic as I furiously tried to dredge up memories of my high school biology.) It took most of the semester—and primarily the public school teacher's active intervention to get her children and my student home safely when a gang battle loomed in the neighborhood—to get this student to broaden her grasp of another's moral strengths. Because I involve students in weekly *oral* reflection sessions as part of the course, I can also count on other students to challenge the morally insensitive rather than my assuming the pulpit of moral authority.

One clear danger in the development of moral sensitivity is that it will also inculcate a sense of moral superiority. We can imagine an all-knowing premed student saying something like, "The Chicago Public School system really does enforce a 'savage inequality.' Thank God I know what a femur is and am committed to making a difference." Here the student defines herself as morally superior not only to the teacher, but to an entire school system and to her fellow premed majors who are not out there helping the poor, neglected children. So, in class we always do two kinds of exercises at various stages. First, we discuss what we are learning from the community leaders and the people we serve. In what concrete ways are we deeply indebted to them? Second, we counteract the tendency always to do a deficit analysis of the communities that we serve by spending one whole reflection session doing an asset-based analysis, in which we discuss nothing but the strengths of the communities and the people we serve.

Moral Judgment. Christina Ferrantelli's family had a long history of involvement with the Salvation Army, so when she asked to do her service as a volunteer on a Salvation Army food truck, I readily agreed. Here is what Christina had to say in one of her reflection essays about her experience:

> We handed out sandwiches and apples and juice to *anyone* who came up to the van. We fed prostitutes, pimps, kids, mechanics, moms, grandmas, homeless guys, crack addicts, and drug dealers. . . . After 4+ hours, I was exhausted and found myself looking forward to getting home. . . .
>
> I don't know about this. I don't think I like this type of community service. It didn't feel good. Well, it felt good to give the kids food knowing that they probably don't have food at home. But no one's life was changed. No one's situation was changed. Perhaps, our feeding program helps people to not change their situation. . . . I also feel distinctly separate from the people that come to the van. *They* come to *our* van and *we* give *them* food. Then *they* go away and *we* go away. We've all got a sense of *us* and *them* and I don't know how to even begin to go about breaking that down. Sometimes there was casual conversation between us. Sometimes there was hostile conversation. But there was never meaningful conversation. . . .
>
> At first, I thought any changes that will take place on the south side must come from public policy. . . . There is a new [program] underway I just learned about from my public policy friend. He told me the area where the feeding program runs has been labeled an official empowerment zone. This means that millions of dollars will be poured into the south side and community members and business owners in the community decide where it will go and what it will be used for. I was skeptical when I heard this because so many similar programs have failed, precisely because they do not attack the real issue, which I believe is racism. I'm seeing its effects first hand. And experiencing racism within myself as I try not to see each person that approaches

our van as a crack addict. But, it looks to me like crack addiction on the south
side is just another branch of the racism tree.

Clearly, Christina is involved in a complex process of moral reasoning,
but it is something other than what Kohlberg's followers mean by reasoning based on moral principles and much closer to *phronesis,* or practical
moral intelligence. Moral principles are involved, to be sure (See also
MacIntyre, 1981, pp. 144–145, 151–152). Christina, for example, is quite
clear about dichotomizing reasoning that separates humans into a *we* and a
they. She thinks systemically about the root causes of poverty. Most important, she is engaged in a self-reflective act of moral judgment ("And experiencing racism within myself"). As Anne Colby and associates put it, "In real
life moral dilemmas do not come neatly packaged like hypothetical dilemmas, which typically involve a given set of simple facts. Almost any real
moral dilemma or question involves significant ambiguity. . . . Thus, in
order to find meaning amid the moral ambiguity of real-life situations, people must develop habits of moral interpretation and intuition through which
they perceive the everyday world" (Colby, Ehrlich, Beaumont, and
Stephens, 2003, p. 106).

Service-learning courses put students precisely in morally ambiguous
contexts that challenge just about any moral framework. The most important consequence of Christina's reflections was that when she read a portion
of her written reflections to the class, she, not I, put all of the issues of a
course on religion and social justice on the table. Developing moral judgment in this approach becomes a collective wading through of all the ambi-
guities that Christina saw. To aid in this process, at one point in such a
course I have the students interview a leader at the community organization
where they are working, asking two questions: "What is your vision of a just
society," and "How do we get there?" Then I ask the students to compare the
responses with their own. "Habits of moral interpretation" are found through
an interactive dialectic of alternative frameworks rather than as a serial development through stages.

Moral Motivation. The literature on moral motivation as a developmental process stresses that the motivation to act on one's moral judgment
depends essentially on the degree to which being moral becomes a core part
of one's identity (Blasi, 1993, 1995). At some point not to act at all and not
to act morally become a violation of one's true self. From this point of view,
asking students what they have learned about themselves through their service becomes an important reflective exercise.

Much of the literature on people who act in a crisis suggests that the
shift from a moral judgment to moral action appears to them as utterly ordinary. Samuel and Pearl Oliner's studies of rescuers of Jews during World
War II indicated that the act of rescue "was less a decision made at a critical juncture than a choice prefigured by an established character and way
of life" (Oliner and Oliner, 1988, p. 222). However, the shift toward action

in younger adults whose identity is still under formation requires both an act of moral imagination and a sense of personal agency.

The right moral action may seem like simply connecting the dots, but leaping from a series of points to a line is a qualitative transformation. Ben Nowicki performed that leap for the entire class of students who had studied the social conditions of third-world poverty on the border of Mexico and Arizona with three DePaul professors. While on the border, we had visited a Fair Trade coffee cooperative in Agua Prieta, Sonora, called Just Coffee. The cooperative linked farmers in Chiapas growing coffee with their fellow villagers who had traveled north in search of work. In Agua Prieta the immigrants grind and roast the coffee beans on buyers' demand and ship the coffee ultra-fresh to customers in the United States. Ben envisioned how students in Chicago could become another link in the chain. He and virtually the entire class researched the literature on Fair Trade and developed their own marketing materials, formed a connection with a local distributor of Fair Trade coffee, segmented the Chicago area, and fanned out in groups to reach every coffee shop in the city.

For Cara Joyce the act of imagination was also an act of self-empowerment. The new possibilities for action and being were brought home to her through her service with an advocacy group that is committed to a Freirean style of popular education (Freire, 1971):

> Of all of the ideas for social change that I was exposed to . . . I think that I have learned the most about what is possible and what is within anyone's grasp at the Interfaith Worker Rights Center. They use the model of popular education to help workers create their own unions, demand benefits and fair wages, and improve their own skill set and attractiveness to employers in their own community. . . . I have only been at the center for a few weeks and feel like I'm just scratching the surface of what their ambitions are and what they get done, but the idea of linking one's personal experience with the larger social systems through education is an amazing tool. . . . If this experience did empower me in any way, I am glad that it showed me that my limits are not as hard-wired and concrete as I thought they were, and that some of my preconceived notions of a good job and a good life need some more examination.

A sense of agency, then, is also critical for the transition to action. Again, the Oliners state it directly: "Rescuers felt that they could control events and shape their own destinies. . . . Rather than regarding themselves as mere pawns . . . , they . . . perceived themselves as actors, capable of making and implementing plans and willing to accept the consequences" (1988, p. 177). It is often the case, as it was for Cara, that the people whom our students serve who are part of active community organizations manage to communicate to students that they too can be agents of change (see, for example, Colby, Ehrlich, Beaumont, and Stephens, 2003, pp. 122–123).

To assist in this process, we do several kinds of reflective exercises in my service-learning classes. "Taking Stock" is one exercise that we do at midterm. Students answer frankly what their most important learning experiences have been and where they are still struggling conceptually. They discuss what kinds of brick walls they have encountered in their service context. I post these without names attached on our electronic discussion board and ask students to assist one another. Developing a sense of community, I have found, enhances the sense of individual agency.

Moral Character. Moral development along this fourth vector in service-learning classes for younger adults lacks one essential component—time. Character is formed over decades, not months. It is important to be modest about one's expectations for a single service-learning class. If liberal education along the entire span of a college career, including various opportunities for experiential education, were a networked process, we might be able to see clearer signs of impact in facilitating a self-determined process of character development. For this to happen the key moral question that would have to be addressed in a variety of ways across the curriculum would be not, "What is the right thing to do?" but "Whom shall I become?" As it stands, Pascarella and Terenzini (2005) conclude that there is little longitudinal evidence to confirm what, if any, impact college has on moral character.

Colby and her associates take a more optimistic view by discussing how the formation of identity and character are connected. Colby cites longitudinal studies of those who have had powerful learning experiences during their college years, such as the Freedom Riders of 1964: "'You learned too much [in Mississippi],'" Colby quotes one veteran as saying, "'to go back to what you were doing before. . . .'" (Colby, Ehrlich, Beaumont, and Stephens, 2003, pp. 188–189). Students like Andrea, Josh, Ben, and Cara who have lived and studied along the border and have engaged in service learning in Chicago as part of their response to what they experienced in Mexico (at DePaul we discuss linking the global to the local) speak the same language as those Freedom Riders. Can we say, then, that moral identity is the DNA for a moral character that evolves over time and in confronting many different challenges?

At this point I suspect some readers may well be asking, "What business is it anyway for colleges to be forming particular moral characters?" My answer is five-fold. First, all education, to the degree that it has any impact, is character forming. Even the most value-neutral course conveys the value of rational inquiry as a guiding principle in human life. Second, if we as educators are always implicitly affecting students' moral development across its four components, we ought to become conscious explicitly of how we are doing so. Third, the liberal arts, as I understand them, are in the business of liberating the potential of students to actualize the good as well as the true and the beautiful. Fourth, openness to a plurality of visions of the good and enabling students to examine alternative visions critically are key to this liberation. Fifth, service-learning courses do not, in fact, lead to uniform visions of the good or to a linear moral development. While their visions of social ills and social justice and the levers of social change may overlap, the students that I have quoted have begun to form their own distinct social perspectives and characters. Andrea, grounded in her self-understanding, sees networked communities built on strong personal relationships as the key to social change. Josh, stemming in part from his human rights work, argues for a counterculture of resistance. Ben, influenced by socially engaged Buddhism, wants to create a "culture of radical awakening" in which "the process of uncovering myself is directly linked to understanding the reality of life for others." Christina probes the roots of racism. And Cara calls for a Freirean form of education exercised inside the campus walls but also in solidarity with struggling workers and migrants. Linear moral development toward a preconceived end simply is not an option in a multiply diverse college classroom even were it a desired goal.

Practice and the Art of Cathedral Building

From a longtime antipoverty worker, Anne Colby draws a metaphor for the kind of civic engagement that service learning hopes to catalyze. This activist "compared himself to the cathedral builders, chipping away at social problems the way stone masons of the Middle Ages inched along in building cathedrals, knowing that the massive churches would not be finished for three or four hundred years" (Colby, Ehrlich, Beaumont, and Stephens, 2003, p. 123). This is a very difficult understanding to convey to students. Students do grasp intuitively that to become good at anything requires time and practice, practice, practice. However, there is an expanded, moral definition of a practice implicit in this metaphor of cathedral builders. Alasdair MacIntyre (1981) presents the classic definition of such a practice: "By a 'practice' I am going to mean any coherent and complex form of socially established cooperative human activity through which goods internal to that form of activity are realized in the course of trying to achieve those standards of excellence which are appropriate to, and partially definitive of, that form of activity, with the result that human powers to achieve excellence and human conceptions of the ends and goals involved are systematically extended" (p. 175).

Stated more simply in terms relevant to our discussion, a practice is the engine of a process that leads from a moral identity to a moral character. A practice, I believe, is also a process that unifies the four components of a moral life.

In a genuine practice one's own core self is always at stake. If we set MacIntyre's definition against the Buddhist epigraph that opened this chapter, we came face-to-face with a paradox: one needs to become a real person, a person of moral integrity and commitment, to find a practice, but a practice is the means by which the internal goods of any activity are reached and the internal good of the self as distinct from its instrumental objectives is generated.

There are many ways in which a service-learning course can instigate a practice. For Josh, writing human rights letters became a practice virtually instantly when he realized that a real person's life was at stake. The instrumental good of improving his writing skills became encapsulated in the internal good of advocating for human rights, "speaking truth to power." Of course, as I have said, a practice takes practice over longer periods of time than a semester.

Practice and Liberation

Martha Nussbaum (1997), drawing from Seneca, argues that historically there have been two conceptions of a liberal education. Both revolve around the word *liberalis,* or "fitted for freedom," as Nussbaum translates it. Fitted for freedom can refer to the initiation of an elite into the traditions of their society, or, as Seneca intended, it can mean the production of free men and women, free "because they can call their minds their own" (p. 293). Again relying on Seneca, Nussbaum sees cultivating humanity as opting for the second meaning while honoring the traditions revered by proponents of the first meaning by critically appropriating those traditions. Such cultivation requires transcending the perspectives and allegiances of one's group and addressing a plurality of visions and traditions both within and outside of one's own cultural location (Nussbaum, 1997). Ultimately, for "cathedral builders," it requires some sense of the transcendent worth of work and action that of necessity will span generations (Colby, Ehrlich, Beaumont, and Stephens, 2003).

There are no twenty-five easy lessons for cultivating humanity in ourselves and others. It requires practice and, arguably, a practice. Nor, as critics of development theories rightfully suggest, is there an irreversible progression along a linear path to a definable goal (see Pascarella and Terenzini, 2005, pp. 48–51). Rather, as Gary Snyder (1990), echoing Zen masters, puts it, "practice *is* the path." Practice "*puts you out there* where the unknown happens, where you encounter surprise" (p. 153; emphasis in the original). The argument for service learning as one pedagogy of engagement can be summarized in Snyder's phrase: it puts students and their teachers out there. It upsets cognitive and moral frameworks, broadens the heart's constrained habits, and enlivens our moral imagination and sense of agency. It challenges our core sense of self. In so doing it energizes the starfish to move along all of its vectors. It is a first step toward the practice that happens when you become a real person.

References

Blasi, A. "The Development of Identity: Some Implications for Moral Functions." In G. G. Noam and T. E. Wren (eds.), *The Moral Self.* Cambridge, Mass.: MIT Press, 1993.

Blasi, A. "Moral Understanding and Moral Personality: The Process of Moral Integration." In W. M. Kurtines and S. L. Gewirtz (eds.), *Moral Development: Introduction.* Boston: Allyn & Bacon, 1995.

Colby, A., Ehrlich, T., Beaumont, E., and Stephens, J. *Educating Citizens: Preparing America's Undergraduates for Lives of Moral and Civic Responsibility.* San Francisco: Jossey-Bass, 2003.

Eyler, J., and Giles, D. E., Jr. *Where's the Learning in Service-Learning?* San Francisco: Jossey-Bass, 1999.

Freire, P. *The Pedagogy of the Oppressed.* New York: Herder and Herder, 1971.

Gilligan, C. *In a Different Voice: Psychological Theory and Women's Development.* Cambridge, Mass.: Harvard University Press, 1982.

Hatcher, J. A., Bringle, R. G., and Muthiah, R. "Designing Effective Reflection: What Matters to Service-Learning?" *Michigan Journal of Community Service Learning,* Fall 2004, *11,* 38–46.

Kohlberg, L. "Stages of Moral Development." In C. Beck, B. Crittenden, and E. Sullivan (eds.), *Moral Education.* Toronto: University of Toronto Press, 1971.

Kohlberg, L. *Essays on Moral Development: Vol. 1. The Philosophy of Moral Development: Moral States and the Idea of Justice.* New York: Harper Collins, 1981.

Kohlberg, L., Levine, C., and Hewer, A. "Moral Stages: The Current Formulation of the Theory." In L. Kohlberg (ed.), *Essays in Moral Development: Vol. 2. The Psychology of Moral Development.* New York: HarperCollins, 1984.

MacIntyre, A. *After Virtue.* Notre Dame, Ind.: University of Notre Dame Press, 1981.

Morton, K. "Making Meaning: Reflections on Community, Service and Learning." In R. Devine, J. A. Favazza, and F. M. McLain (eds.), *From Cloister to Commons: Concepts and Models for Service-Learning in Religious Studies.* Washington, D.C.: American Association for Higher Education, 2002.

Narváez, D., and Rest, J. "The Four Components of Acting Morally." In W. Kurtines and J. Gewirtz (eds.), *Moral Behavior and Moral Development: An Introduction.* New York: McGraw-Hill, 1995.

Nussbaum, M. C. *Cultivating Humanity: A Classical Defense of Reform in Liberal Education.* Cambridge, Mass.: Harvard University Press, 1997.

Oliner, S. P., and Oliner, P. M. *The Altruistic Personality: Rescuers of Jews in Nazi Europe.* New York: Free Press, 1988.

Pascarella, E. T., and Terenzini, P. T. *How College Affects Students: Volume Two, A Third Decade of Research.* San Francisco: Jossey-Bass, 2005.

Rest, J., Narváez, D., Bebeau, M., and Thoma, S. *Postconventional Moral Thinking: A Neo-Kohlbergian Approach.* Mahwah, N.J.: Erlbaum, 1999.

Snyder, G. *The Practice of the Wild.* San Francisco: North Point Press, 1990.

CHARLES R. STRAIN is associate vice president for academic affairs and professor of religious studies at DePaul University.

A residential learning community that melds academic affairs and student affairs concerns can address the whole student through fostering liberal learning experiences. Students can explore innovative and controversial ideas and activities designed to challenge their personal and intellectual growth in a community of faculty and student affairs staff who encourage, value, and support open exchange.

The Zen of Unit One: Residential Learning Communities Can Foster Liberal Learning at Large Universities

Howard K. Schein

In the winter of 1962 I hopped onto the Rock Island Railroad with a footlocker and a duffel bag. I rode from Chicago to Grinnell, Iowa, to spend four years engaged in a liberal arts education. I was a product of the Chicago public school system on my way to explore the academic unknown. Fifteen years later, when I began my 28-plus years as director of Unit One Living-Learning Program at the University of Illinois, Urbana-Champaign, the direction I took in developing a large living-learning program was largely and unconsciously shaped by my upbringing at a small, liberal arts college. I did not explicitly set out to recreate my undergraduate experience for the ten thousand or so students who have participated in Unit One. I'm sure that I was winging it for my first ten years. But I'm also sure that the values that I wrestled with developing at Grinnell College have been strongly embedded in my thinking about what an undergraduate education should be. Consequently, in my attempt to create a setting where my undergraduate experience can be attained on a large, Research-I university campus, I have focused on the basic values of a liberal education.

Basic Structure of Unit One

Unit One is a residentially based academic program. Generally classified as a residential learning community (RLC) and specifically as a living-learning center (LLC), Unit One, housed in Allen Residence Hall on the University of Illinois, Urbana-Champaign campus, was founded in 1972 with the charge of creating an academic program in a university residence hall. Through an evolutionary growth process, Unit One has developed to be a program that gives undergraduate students the opportunity to have the experience of a small, liberal arts college at a large, Research-I university.

Unit One is superimposed onto and integrated into the residence hall structure. Unit One's core staff consists of a director, assistant director, office manager, two art instructors, two music program coordinators, and three undergraduate program advisors. Core staff are appointed either by the housing division or by their teaching departments with Unit One funds. The resident director and the area coordinator of Allen Residence Hall are also part of the Unit One core staff. This staff is responsible for administering Unit One's academic and non-credit-granting programs. Along with the core staff is a revolving teaching staff of about sixty instructors from various university departments.

Unit One has several basic programmatic features:

Academic: About seventy-five different credit-granting courses are taught each year. About fifty courses are taught each semester. Half of these fifty courses are taught for one semester only; the other half are repeated each semester.

Music instruction: One specific course provides private music lessons to about 180 students each semester.

Guests-in-residence: About six to eight guests are invited to spend one to two weeks in residency at Unit One. Guests live in an Allen Hall suite and engage with students in classes, in scheduled presentations, and in informal conversations and activities.

Non-credit programming, including topical discussions, documentary film showings, guest speakers, field trips, volunteer activities, and recitals.

The facilities that support these features have been built into the Unit One infrastructure, ranging from seven Internet-wired seminar classrooms and two large multipurpose spaces for classes and activities to studios for photography, ceramics, and electronic music and office space for faculty and staff (a more detailed description is at http://www.housing.uiuc.edu/living/unit1).

Liberal Education at Residential Learning Communities

My daughter is now a freshman at Grinnell, so I've paid special attention to how that school identifies itself. Its academic planning booklet (Grinnell, 2004–2005) puts forth their version of a liberal arts education:

> A liberal arts education has at its center four things that distinguish it from
> other kinds of learning: critical thinking, continuing examination of life,

encounters with difference, and the free exchange of ideas. By offering an education in the liberal arts, Grinnell College endorses lifelong learning characterized by sustained intellectual curiosity and an open mind for assessing the
unfamiliar. At the same time, by using critical thinking to assess evidence, to
identify assumptions, to test logic, to reason correctly, and to take responsibility for the conclusions and actions that result, a student of the liberal arts
can grow personally as well as intellectually. A liberally educated person
should be capable of principled judgment, seeking to understand the origins,
context, and implications of any area of study, rather than looking exclusively
at its application [p. 2].

Small, liberal arts colleges are structured to attain these goals. Faculty
are hired to be teacher-scholars and they are rewarded for good, interactive
teaching. Students who attend these schools have similar educational expectations, and these students are also likely to share similar values. At large
Research-I schools, working toward a liberal education is problematic: faculty's role in regard to undergraduate interaction and teaching is usually
ambiguous; the goals of professional education in non-liberal arts curricula
sometimes run contrary to the goals of liberal education; the large size of
the undergraduate population, combined with the multiplicity of undergraduates' educational agendas, present many problems in working toward
the ideals of academic intimacy. Residential learning communities are
designed to address these difficulties. In *Making the Most of College,* Richard
Light (2001) alludes to the strengths of residential settings when he points
out that "learning outside of classes, especially in residential settings and
extracurricular activities such as the arts, is vital."

Residential Learning Community Structure and
Campus Structure

Residential learning communities are academic programs housed in residence
halls. These programs usually have a developmental underpinning, they frequently incorporate academic themes or courses, and they frequently are
structured in response to their campus's specific needs. Residential learning
communities serve many purposes. In some cases, they are constructed to
address specific areas of academic inquiry (for example, they congregate specific curricula), or to address students' academic skills needs (for example,
they congregate students who need specific support services), or to address
students' extracurricular interests (such as wellness or community service).

On campuses where these programs are found, an underlying agenda
for residential learning communities is tied to the concept of student success. Criteria for the learning communities' successes are consequently
based on data that reflect measurable variables, such as retention in college
or in specified curricula, grade point, reasonable progress toward gradua-
tion, adjustment to college, and timely choosing of a major.

Unit One is constructed differently. It was designed as a model for any Research-I institution to provide a setting that supports the kind of liberal learning agendas that usually characterize small, liberal arts colleges. Unit One's underlying agenda is not tied to such outcomes as grade point, adjustment to college, or retention and progress toward degree. Rather, Unit One's agenda is tied to the less easily quantified criterion of "quality of education," an underlying rationale for a liberal learning experience. We take for granted that the qualities of a liberal education are desirable to incorporate into undergraduates' educations. We also know that measuring successful outcomes is difficult, especially since many of these hoped-for outcomes are set in motion during students' undergraduate years and unveil themselves over lifetimes. "Quality-of-education" programs are risky ventures if these programs are held responsible for data-driven success, since objectively measurable outcomes are difficult to track. Success for programs like Unit One depends on administrations that accept qualitative data, largely in the form of faculty and student feedback.

For most residential learning communities, cosponsorship between the academic and student affairs branches of the campus (the latter usually through the housing division) is critical. On small campuses, this cosponsorship is usually collegial because all arms of the campus administration and the faculty are focused on the same goal: students' development in their academic and personal realms. On large campuses, however, where the faculty and student affairs agendas are not always coincidental, good working relationships are usually difficult to negotiate, maintain, and manage.

Student Affairs and Faculty Relationships

Student affairs operations tend to follow a linearly hierarchical model of the sort found in the corporate world. Campuses' student affairs philosophies, which typically are supportive of students' academic development, filter down uniformly through student affairs divisions, and accountability to specific points of supervision is very clearly recognized. Student affairs usually runs its sponsorship of residential learning communities through their housing divisions, where staff hierarchies and accountability are clearly delineated. If for no other reason than legal liability, this kind of accountability makes sense. Students' personal well-being is largely the responsibility of student affairs through living arrangements, campus health centers, campus recreation centers, and student entertainment venues. Whereas we don't frequently see court cases that revolve around professors brainwashing their students, we do see lawsuits that evolve from hazing, drinking, and date rape. (See Kuh, 1983, for a more detailed discussion of student affairs issues.)

Faculty operate quite differently from the student affairs model. Under the academic affairs umbrella, faculty try to pay little attention to administrative lines of report and behave more like independent contractors with dual allegiances, one to their departments and one to their disciplines (see, for example, Weingartner, 1996). Faculty do have lines of report, but accountability within these lines is quite different from accountability that characterizes student affairs. With research being high on most Research-I faculty's priority lists, institutional lines of reporting are but one of several places toward which faculty must orient their behavior. Because their disciplinary colleagues largely judge faculty's academic worth, one set of faculty fealties is focused outside of their institutions and toward their national and international academic disciplinary peers. And because academic freedom promotes many different lines of thinking within departments and because disciplinary philosophies within departments and institutions are not necessarily uniform, faculty do not tend to toe a departmental or institutional line in the same way that their student affairs colleagues do.

At my institution, for instance, the housing division has a mission statement that is printed on the back of the picture identification cards that staff wear around their necks, and the department of residence life in the housing division has a vision statement, "Growing, Learning, and Mattering, for every person, on every floor, in every community." These mission and vision statements are actively invoked as the conceptual foundations that guide the creation of policies and programs, and we are frequently asked to rationalize how given actions are consistent with this mission or vision. One would be hard pressed to find a comparable statement that faculty attend to at any Research-I institution.

Student affairs tends to make solid commitments to making sure that positions that are key to programmatic success are staffed. If, for instance, the housing division creates the position of program coordinator of a residential learning community, the odds are great that, despite staff rollover, the position will be filled. If a faculty member commits to teaching a course at a residential learning community, that faculty's commitment is not likely to last more than several semesters; faculty work agendas are ever changing—new committee work, new departmental administrative assignments, sabbaticals, changing teaching obligations, and more all cycle into faculty's long-term schedules. And when a particular faculty leaves an RLC, replacement is usually problematic. Finding a new and appropriate person from within the faculty ranks to cycle into this teaching slot may be difficult, especially since this person must come from within the ranks of existing faculty who may or may not have the time, expertise, or inclination to participate in the RLC.

This raises the issue of teaching personnel. Many RLCs use instructors other than regular faculty—adjunct faculty, graduate teaching assistants, and departmental instructors who are not on a tenure track. In some cases, RLCs are convenient teaching assignments for spousal hires who do not want or who cannot get regular, tenure-track assignments. Hiring instructors who are not on a tenure track presents interesting issues: The absence of regular faculty can be a flag that the faculty are not interested in the RLC concept. Critics may contend that the level of instruction at RLCs is subpar. How Unit One addresses this issue is the topic of the next section.

How Unit One Assesses Instructional Issues

Campus policy assigns issues of course and instructor credibility to the colleges and departments that offer instruction at Unit One. Instructors are appointed to teach Unit One courses under the guidelines that the instructor's department uses to make any of its appointments. As well, when we construct topical, experimental, or noncurricular courses to be taught specifically at Unit One, the department under whose rubric these courses are offered must approve these courses. In this way, Unit One's academic offerings are consistent with campus instructional policies.

Unit One utilizes teaching personnel who represent all levels of instructors, including TAs, adjuncts, and regular faculty. TAs and adjunct instructors typically teach courses and discussion sections of large lectures that repeat on a regular basis. Regular faculty are usually found at Unit One teaching a revolving group of first-year seminars. These faculty are recruited on a yearly basis.

Adjuncts and advanced TAs teach our experimental, noncurricular, and topical seminars under the umbrella of Unit One Extra Options. These one- or two-credit-hour seminars have several key features: They are graded on a pass-fail option; their topics change in response to instructor and student requests; and they are meant to be small, highly interactive groups of five to fifteen students with a good deal of student-instructor interaction. In some cases, these seminars are outgrowths of regular courses where the instructor can take the course beyond the syllabus (for example, for the ethics course the seminar could be the Ethics of Dissent; and for the child psychology course, the seminar could be Exploring Parenting and Family Processes). In some cases these seminars are stand-alone (such as American Sign Language for the Deaf or the Roots of Popular Music); in some cases we introduce service-learning through these seminars (such as Art and Social Action; Volunteer Projects at Local Elementary Schools).

When TAs teach these seminars, they design their courses under the supervision of departmental faculty members, with oversight by the Unit One director. This seminar series has given many advanced graduate students a way to design and teach their own courses and is seen and used by departments as another vehicle to prepare their advanced students for the rigors of teaching in the profession. An added advantage to graduate students who teach these seminars at Unit One and who are looking for small-college teaching positions is a valid resume addition that reflects knowledge of a model of teaching generally found at a small, liberal arts college.

Bridging the Waters Between Student and Academic Affairs Philosophies

Although in the large-campus model student affairs is split from academic affairs, students certainly don't envision their lives with this split. For students, their lives are whole entities with emotional, physical, and intellectual concerns wrapped into one interactive package. Addressing this package as a unified venture is one of the strengths of a residentially based academic program, where the various aspects of students' lives can be integrated.

In this context, residence halls on large campuses are interesting places. They are loaded with affect and short on intellectuality. For many students, residence halls represent their safe place, where they can retreat from the challenges of their academic experiences. For many students, this retreat divorces them from the intellectual rigors they find in the academic interactions that characterize many modern classrooms. Surely, students study in their residence halls, and surely, they form study groups to help them master their curricular course material. Although most modern residence halls put a lot of effort into co-curricular activities, most residence halls are not places where students are encouraged to stretch their intellectual capabilities. In observing that campuses address diversity issues mainly through student affairs efforts, Levine (1994) makes this observation about faculty involvement in students' lives outside of the classroom: "The co-curriculum, though rich in diversity programs, lacks intellectual depth, is unconnected with the academic side of higher education, and is largely ignored by the faculty " (p. 341). Although this observation targets co-curricular diversity programming, it can probably also be generalized to faculty's involvement in all of the co-curriculum. Basically, when interacting with undergraduates, faculty tend to focus on classroom activities. Their lack of involvement in other student activities leaves a gaping hole of possible involvement in helping students become liberally educated and in helping students to address their everyday concerns with intellectual tools alongside their affective tools.

The challenge, then, is to work with the affect that runs so strongly in residence halls and manipulate it in a way that accomplishes two tasks: making these settings intellectually safe, and including instruction or programming that inserts an intellectual component into this safe setting.

Students are perfectly adept at constructing community. Most freshmen seek to construct social networks, especially ones in which they are comfortable, and upperclass students are constantly refining their networks. But these networks are most frequently built around social, not academic, concerns. Providing an intellectual component into this social sphere is the beginning of expanding the process of becoming liberally educated into the everyday lives of our students. Residence halls can provide a setting where students may feel safe to take the kinds of chances they need to stimulate their intellectual growth.

Challenge and Support: A Basic Model to Instigate Change

A very basic model for effecting student change involves both challenge and support. Stimulus for change comes from the challenge of confronting and dealing with uncomfortable situations, newness, difference, and so forth. The challenge is to confront this discomfort in a way that effects change. Change can come in many forms, not all of which are immediately apparent. Among the kinds of changes we hope to see are new attitudes, new ways of thinking, new ways of communicating, new behaviors, and the like.

In a residence hall setting, challenge is all over the place. Without outside interjection, basic challenges to students come in the form of dealing with a large group of peers in a communal-living setting. For many students, for instance, merely dealing with roommates for the first time in their lives is an adjustment. As well, students face the new challenge of dealing with a host of peers' ideas about how one's life should be lived and the differing moral and ethical stances that drive peers' behaviors in the context of living without constant parental supervision. Moreover, of course, dealing with the chaos and noise that pervade residence halls is always an issue. These situations are basic to any university residence hall experience.

In this setting, support comes from staff's ability to mediate interactions and from students' ability to retreat to comfort zones of the known and the familiar. Built into this scenario are mechanisms to help make these situations emotionally and physically safe, and, in most cases, students find sanctuary in their peer communities and in their rooms.

Missing, in most cases, is challenge from the intellectual realm, the insertion of ideas that do not come from what is inherent in peer interactions but that come from the outside. Also missing in most residence halls is staff pressing students to explore, more deeply than students usually would, the newness that they confront in their everyday lives. This is the void that living-learning communities can fill.

Unit One—A Case Study

Unit One Living-Learning Program was established at the University of Illinois as a model for undergraduates to engage in the liberal learning process. It was established by the chancellor with a broad yet vague mandate of exploring the feasibility of an academic program in a residential setting. The leadership of Unit One was given a pretty broad range of possibilities. As Unit One has grown and evolved, it has always kept several objectives on the table: to provide an eclectic offering of courses and non-credit programming; to provide a safe place for students' personal and intellectual growth; to provide a variety of avenues to explore ideas and activities that are new, innovative, and controversial; and to provide a community that values and supports an open exchange of ideas with a cadre of faculty and student affairs staff who encourage and support these goals.

More than 80 percent of Unit One students tend to be freshmen and sophomores (who tend to be a representative sample of enrollment in the university's colleges and majors), so we incorporate into our mission an attempt to jump-start students on their way toward making good use of the university and its resources.

When I describe Unit One to prospective students, I frequently describe the program in two different ways: the list and the demeanor. The list is an outline of our activities and facilities—our guarantees (for example, we guarantee credit courses, music lessons, guests-in-residence, and facilities). But the demeanor of the hall is central to most students' experiences and is the backbone of the program's success. The community that is recreated by each year's students provides the fluidity of interaction and openness of communication that allows Unit One's mission to be actualized.

Unit One's Operating Structure

At the University of Illinois, Urbana-Champaign, the housing division is the primary sponsor of residential learning communities, but the provost's office plays a very integrated role. With this level of support and freedom, I have been able to be extremely flexible and opportunistic in making use of campus resources.

We have figured out a way to integrate the faculty and student affairs models that I previously described in order to make best use of faculty and student affairs staffs. We ask faculty to do what faculty do best with undergraduates: teach. We then ask student affairs staff to do what they expect to do: support the academic mission of the institution. Finally, we ask faculty and student affairs staff to collaborate when appropriate situations arise. Students respond most reliably to faculty expertise in the classroom, and faculty's role in promoting students' intellectual development demands an ongoing and reliable commitment over time by students. In Unit One, we then extend the classroom into the students' noncurricular lives.

The academic affairs-student affairs dichotomy has never been a problem at Unit One. Rather than designing programs that necessarily ask for real-time collaboration, the housing staff and the faculty each make use of the contributions to the environment that the other makes: faculty teach students who live in an environment that encourages students to exchange ideas in a free and open setting; consequently, housing staff get to conduct discussions with students who have issues of an academic nature in the context of affective and personal developmental issues.

Sometimes we get lucky and intentionally design programs integrating academic teaching and student affairs programming collaboration. A good example of this liberal learning potential revolved around a field trip of about forty-five students to see the musical, *Miss Saigon*, in Chicago. Prior to the trip, a Unit One political science instructor who teaches a course on the Vietnam War presented a program and film to explain the context of the musical. Once in Chicago, another Unit One instructor with a specialty in opera production arranged for a backstage tour, and the trip coordinator arranged for the students to eat at a Vietnamese restaurant after the performance. Even helping the bus driver recover from several wrong turns was educational.

Since the residence hall is the place where the basis of all of this action occurs, and since academic staff are, in a sense, visitors in this setting, the main responsibility falls in the lap of the residence hall and living-learning center core staff to maintain an environment that supports the intervention of academic staff. Rather than seeing academic staff as interlopers, this academic staff is best viewed as close and welcome family members who have keys to the house, their own guest rooms, and unrestricted refrigerator privileges.

With this access to the setting, instructors have several routes to creating interaction with their students: small class size; seminar-style classrooms; instructor office space; faculty meal passes to facilitate eating with students; budgets to support out-of-class ventures; honoraria to thank instructors for extra work; and more.

With their extra funds, instructors are encouraged to hold extra class meetings to facilitate review of material, film showings that complement in-class discussions, field trips both on and off campus, meals at international restaurants, inviting students to instructors' homes, and so on. Moreover, at times instructors open their course activities (such as film showings or field trips) to all members of the living-learning community.

A critical feature, probably the most important, is students' own feeling of entitlement. Students as well as staff always have the ability to create programming that addresses the issues that interest them. At Unit One, students can readily form student groups that have long-term agendas and regular meetings, and students can also program one-time events that address specific topics. From student initiatives and from student groups, students have developed programming ranging from chess to a weekly film forum called Couch Potatoes, from ceramics exploration to Small Town America, a group that takes field trips to visit small midwestern towns. All of these involve Unit One staff and faculty.

The content, both academically and programmatically, is eclectic because we do not have a decided curricular bent. We feel that the process of intellectual interchange is at least as important, if not more important, than the content. Unit One has, however, paid special attention to the arts and issues of social concern, both in courses and in non-credit programming, because these two areas appeal universally to our students, regardless of major, and because students engage in these areas very readily. What grows from these efforts is a group of staff who all contribute to students' personal and intellectual growth in a setting where all staff members can contribute what they do best and what they are trained to do. The result is a vibrant community where ideas flow in classes and in planned programming and in the everyday conversations among students.

Unit One's model is to create our version of a small, liberal arts community where all members buy into the basic notion that lively discourse is an important feature of education, where all members see value in participating in this community, and where all members contribute to this community in ways consistent with their vision of the community. But community members are not asked to take a singularly agreed-upon route toward our ultimate goal of promoting lively intellectual interchange, and with this freedom of integrating various styles of approaching the process of education, diverse ideas and educational strategies thrive.

What Students and Faculty Report

At Unit One we solicit semesterly feedback from our faculty, and we have been formally evaluated many times. Some of the richest data have come from instructor interviews and from student focus groups (Grayson, 2003). In Grayson's study, instructors and students discuss the strength of the community as one of the central features of Unit One.

A summary of instructor comments from Grayson's draft of this study includes the following:

(a) Students in living and learning communities have a high level of commitment toward learning. They are eager to engage in open discussion and are full of questions. They are active learners.

(b) Students are rich in their academic backgrounds, interests, ethnicities and cultures.

(c) Smaller class sizes offer many benefits in terms of student engagement, learning and teaching effectiveness.

(d) Living and learning communities have higher levels of community spirit.

(e) Students feel comfortable in their communities and easily make friends with other students.

(f) Students and faculty feel comfortable with each other and have quality interactions.

(g) Living and learning communities foster critical thinking and problem solving through innovative and creative teaching strategies. [Grayson, 2003, p. 13]

One faculty member, who also supervised teaching assistants, pointed out several major differences between teaching at Unit One and at the university at large:

Really knowing your students, having lunch with students, knowing their names, knowing what they want and [what] their personal and professional goals are, establishing meaningful relationships with students, more opportunities to guide or suggest other classes or courses, ability to develop comfortable relationships.

. . . [Unit One] protects the notion of a liberal arts community where teachers and students can engage in meaningful dialogue and reap benefits of intellectual, personal, and professional growth. . . . The larger University context does not easily allow for or promote opportunities for meaningful and comfortable relationships with students to be established or nurtured. [Grayson, 2003, pp. 14–29]

Other faculty comments include the following:

"The community aspect is certainly part of it."

"I lectured on civil rights to a mixed, diverse group and I couldn't shut them up. Unit One builds a sense of community."

"The interaction with the students is better than I have experienced elsewhere so far. They are ready to discuss, interrupt me to ask questions, and also indicate issues they wish to know more about. We always have discussions and everyone talks."

"[Students are] engaged in discussion with openness and candor."

The comfort level is high. ". . . a much higher level of engagement with its students. . . "

"Students at Unit One know each other and feel comfortable in sharing ideas and are very willing to engage in discussion. . . . Students speak up and are not afraid to ask questions. . . . Student engagement, interactive classrooms and open dialogue allow for the exchange of ideas and critical thinking."

"By students' living together, classes congeal faster. Students are together already so they are more likely to do things together . . . care for one another more. . . .They are not overly polite in discussion . . . they take care of details, share material with other kids who miss class." [Grayson, 2003, pp. 14–29]

In other evaluations, instructors who teach two sections of the same course, one at Unit One and one "on campus," frequently comment that the test scores of both sections are usually comparable but that the level of intellectual engagement found in Unit One sections is usually much greater.

Students' responses in focus groups complement the faculty's observations. In Grayson (2003), a summary of students' responses includes the following:

(a) Learning takes place in the entire community. It extends outside of the classroom.
(b) Making connections is easier and one feels more comfortable with other students.
(c) Smaller classrooms offer multiple benefits.
(d) Faculty and instructors are more engaging, more thoughtful and fun.
(e) Living and learning communities offer a variety of benefits not available in other residential halls. [Grayson, 2003, p. 17]

In these focus groups, students commented that their learning carries over outside the classroom; that taking classes with people they know makes it easier to approach each other; that knowing classmates makes the class more comfortable; that collaboration outside of class is common; students experience more respect for classmates who are hallmates; personal relationships between classmates and with instructors make classes more comfortable and open; teachers have respect for students and that dynamic carries over; when students get to know their faculty well, faculty expect more, and they know what they can expect from students; in Unit One, learning is not just about scores, but about participation and involvement and thinking and questioning.

When queried about having conversations across lines of difference, students first identified difference in more dimensions than the standard race-gender-ethnicity boundaries. They saw all nature of difference worthy of noting:

"Everyone . . . has opinions . . . some students are to the right and others to the left and they clash. This is good because we enlighten each other."
"Everyone has different views and much to offer. All the students here are willing to learn and willing to share."
"The idea of respect is a big part of Allen Hall . . . in your classroom, in your room, or in the hallway. I can fall asleep any time of the day [because the noise level is kept at a respectful level]." [Grayson, 2003, p. 21]

When queried about the uniqueness of Unit One and Allen Hall, students offered the following:

- "The small school feeling. To have a unique experience with faculty."
- "Eases the transition from high school to college."
- "You go to Allen Hall, not to a room number. Allen Hall is your identity and it feels good."
- "It (Allen Hall) gives you an identity."
- "It is important for freshmen to have a community; a place that is home and Allen provides that. I cannot emphasize the importance of this." [Grayson, 2003, p. 23]

Unit One Student Identity

One theme that has repeated itself over Unit One's existence is students' identification as campus outsiders (Horwitz, 1989). In fact, for many years we were the outsiders in the minds of much of the campus administration. Not until the campus was called to task to show innovation in undergraduate education did Unit One fall into mainstream campus favor. Now, with residential learning communities experiencing a national growth spurt, we have become a model for others. Although an outside threat can never be maintained as the force that coalesces a community, I think that Unit One students' being consistently identified as outsiders serves the same function.

Unit One students have always been labeled, both by themselves and by the undergraduate campus culture. Over time, they have been the hippies, the campus radicals, the Goths, the alternative lifestylers, the geeks, and more, all of which have been outsider labels. We have never done a political spectrum survey, but, contrary to campus perceptions, I'd bet that our population is actually pretty representative of campus norms on many attitude variables. However, the fact that these students live in a setting that values openness allows them to speak their minds, and their ideas and topics of discussion don't always fall within the boundaries of what other students see as normal.

I'm always drawn to Luna Lovegood, a character in *Harry Potter and the Order of the Phoenix* (J. K. Rowling's 2003 book) who is viewed as a weirdo and an outsider until her special abilities are finally noticed. When my daughter went off to college, my main piece of advice (after suggesting she get to know her professors, of course) was to get to know the Luna Lovegoods of her campus. Getting to know new, and maybe even seemingly strange people and to expose oneself to new ideas is one of the strengths of Unit One. The openness of the environment appears to be one of the underlying features of Unit One that our graduating seniors focused on. This feature reminds me of a statement made in 1952 by Adlai E. Stevenson, former Governor of Illinois: "My definition of a free society is a society where it is safe to be unpopular." (http://www.quotegarden.com/freedom.html). For me, this thought translates into fostering a setting where students feel free to speak their minds without fear of recrimination, even if they voice unpopular sentiments. In this vein, for instance, students take great pride in holding forums that address the conflicting views of evangelical Christians and atheists. Here, discussions of the kinds of opposing views that permeate these students' everyday lives can be held without acrimony or divisiveness.

In May 2004, we invited all of our graduating seniors to dinner. Most had been living in apartments for the previous two years. About fifty stopped by. We asked them to comment on how Unit One fulfilled its promise of providing a liberal education: critical thinking; self understanding; diversity; testing their points of view; ethical, moral, and intellectual development. The following comments on that subject are from these students:

"The strangest people can fit in and feel comfortable. . . . Being with 'weird' people is good."
"We are known as 'weird'—but we're the ones who open themselves freely, think outside the box, and recognize that 'normal' can be 'average.'"
"A place like Allen Hall is intellectually stimulating to me, largely because the culture of openness fostered a great many diverse friendships that helped to grow me as a person."
"[I was] free to express my ideas and opinions. . . . "

Students who move into Allen Hall from other halls frequently cite the difference between Unit One-Allen Hall and other residence halls on campus. One senior reflected:

"The difference between my original residence hall and Allen Hall was drastic. The Unit One environment brought people together . . . and encouraged candid and insightful discussions about pertinent and useful topics. I feel as though I had a chance to develop further as an aware individual, more so than I would elsewhere on this often closed-minded and stifling campus."

This student wasn't aware of the paradigm of the academic affairs-student affairs dichotomy, but she did observe: "Allen's strength lies in the fact that it fosters all aspects of life. Instead of focusing on [credit] hour accumulation, the focus is placed on the total quality of life."

Conclusion

Small, liberal arts colleges have the ability to craft a mission that all members of the faculty and staff buy into and that students recognize as the guiding principle underlying their undergraduate education. Very frequently, the philosophy underlying these principles involves providing these students with a liberal education. By their nature, large Research-I universities are fractionated. No single principle unites the faculty, staff, and student body to guide them in a specific educational direction. For those members of this community who strive to experience a liberal education, residential learning communities can be constructed to approximate the setting of a small, liberal arts college. In these settings, students can get a level of intellectual intensity in their everyday lives, both in and out of the classroom, that integrates their academic and personal development.

Unit One offers a model residential learning community with the mission of nurturing a liberal education for lower-division undergraduates on a large, Research-I campus. The success of Unit One comes from students' buying into the concept that intellectual growth and the lively exchange of ideas are important. But it also comes from the staff members, who foster a community that welcomes the addition of intellectual challenge and who fuel this community with ideas and activities that challenge students to confront the dissonance that these new ideas place into their lives. Fostering community involves conveying an attitude that this community values intellectual engagement. Fostering community involves incorporating concepts like support, acceptance of difference, the value of lively discourse, and willingness to introduce new ideas into the classroom, into non-credit programming, and into the social structure of students' everyday lives in the residence hall. These concepts are readily modeled in the classroom and in purposefully structured non-credit programming. They are also readily modeled in the way staff help students negotiate their everyday relationships. With a little bit of luck, these concepts then become incorporated into the students' long-term community traditions and passed down through student generations.

Fueling this kind of community involves staff's insertion of ideas and challenges that fall outside most students' normal experiences. Students are good at recycling what they know, but they need help to push into the unknown. When students experience new ideas and challenges within the context of a supportive academic community that encourages engagement, they grow. It could be that simple!

References

Grayson, T. E. "Evaluation of Living and Learning Communities, University of Illinois at Urbana-Champaign." Unpublished paper. Urbana: University of Illinois at Urbana-Champaign, Office of the Vice Chancellor for Student Affairs, 2003.

Grinnell College. *Academic Planning for First-Year Students: A Guide to the Liberal Arts at Grinnell College, 2004–2005.* Grinnell, Iowa: Grinnell College, 2004.

Horwitz, H. L. "The Changing Student Culture: A Retrospective." *Educational Record,* 1989, *70,* 24–29.

Kuh, G. D. (ed.). *Understanding Student Affairs Organizations.* New Directions for Student Services, no. 23. San Francisco: Jossey-Bass, 1983.

Levine, A. "Diversity on Campus." In Levine, A. (ed.), *Higher Learning in America: 1980–2000.* Baltimore: Johns Hopkins Press, 1994.

Light, R. J. *Making the Most of College: Students Speak Their Minds.* Cambridge, Mass.: Harvard University Press, 2001.

Weingartner, R. H. *Fitting Form to Function: A Primer on the Organization of Academic Institutions.* Phoenix: The Oryx Press/The American Council on Education, 1996.

HOWARD K. SCHEIN is director of Unit One Living-Learning Program and an adjunct associate professor of higher education in the Department of Educational Organization and Leadership at the University of Illinois, Urbana-Champaign.

INDEX

AAAS. See American Association for the Advancement of Science
Academic inquiry, 13
Adb-El-Khalik, F., 54
Afghanistan, 44, 45, 48
Ahmed, L., 43, 44
Allen Residence Hall (University of Illinois, Urbana-Champaign), 73, 74, 85, 87
American Association for the Advancement of Science (AAAS), 52, 53, 55
Anderson, J. A., 23
Anomalies, 11, 13
Antigone and Its Moral (Eliot), 31
Antigone (Sophocles), 29–33, 35
Aristotle, 5
Arizona, 68
Assignment design, art of, 23–36
Association of American Colleges and Universities (AAC&U), 7, 8
Aurelius, M., 5
Authentic engagement, recognizing, 32–33

Barrera, A., 63, 64
Bartholomae, D., 36
Bean, J., 24
Beaumont, E., 42, 61–63, 67–70
Bebeau, M., 63–65
Benchmarks for Science Literacy (American Association for the Advancement of Science), 55
Beyond the Culture Wars (Graff), 18
Blasi, A., 67
Bloom, A., 4, 7, 8
Bolingbroke, Lord, 42
Booth, W. C., 23, 24, 26, 34
Bramble, J., 51
Breihan, J. E., 42
Bringle, R. G., 62
Bruner, J., 34
Buddhism, 70, 71
Burch, K., 18–20

Carnegie Academy, 36
Cathedral building, 70–71
Character, moral, 69–70
Chiapas, Mexico, 68

Chicago, 68, 69, 73, 81; Public School System, 66
Chicago Religious Leadership Network (CRLN), 65
Clueless in Academe (Graff), 4
Colby, A., 42, 61–63, 67–71
Crawford, B. A., 54
Creon, 30–32, 35
Crisis, 11–13
Critical literacy: fostering, 23–36; and model of ill-structured problems, 24–25; from reading to writing in, 26–32; and recognizing authentic engagement, 24–25; student development and, 25–26
CRLN. See Chicago Religious Leadership Network
Crossfire, 39, 43
Cultivating Humanity (Nussbaum), 4

Dachau, 29
DePaul University, 65, 68, 69
Diogenes, 4
Dualism, 26

Ehrlich, T., 42, 61–63, 67–71
Elbow, P., 25, 26, 36
Eliot, G., 31
Engelmann, B., 29–34, 36
English teachers, 23
Expectancies, forms of, 11, 12
Eyler, J., 61–63

Ferrantelli, C., 66, 67, 69, 70
First Democracy: The Challenge of an Ancient Idea (Woodruff), 41
Forms of expectancies, 11, 12
Forms of Intellectual and Ethical Development in the College Years (Perry), 12, 25, 26
Foucault, M., 5
Freedom Riders, 69
Freire, P., 68, 70

Geertz, C., 7, 8
Genre, understanding, 32
Giles, D. E., Jr., 61–63
Gilligan, C., 21, 63, 64

Back Issue/Subscription Order Form

Copy or detach and send to:

Jossey-Bass, A Wiley Imprint, 989 Market Street, San Francisco CA 94103-1741

Call or fax toll-free: Phone 888-378-2537 6:30AM – 3PM PST; Fax 888-481-2665

Back Issues: Please send me the following issues at $29 each
(Important: please include ISBN number with your order.)

_____

_____

_____

$ _____   Total for single issues

$ _____   SHIPPING CHARGES: SURFACE   Domestic Canadian
                                    First Item $5.00 $6.00
                                    Each Add'l Item $3.00 $1.50
                  For next-day and second-day delivery rates, call the number listed above.

Subscriptions   Please __ start __ renew my subscription to *New Directions for Teaching and Learning* for the year 2___ at the following rate:

U.S.   __ Individual $80   __ Institutional $170
Canada   __ Individual $80   __ Institutional $210
All Others   __ Individual $104   __ Institutional $244
Online subscriptions available too!
**For more information about online subscriptions visit
www.interscience.wiley.com**

$ _____   Total single issues and subscriptions (Add appropriate sales tax for your state for single issue orders. No sales tax for U.S. subscriptions. Canadian residents, add GST for subscriptions and single issues.)

__Payment enclosed (U.S. check or money order only)
__VISA __ MC __ AmEx #_____ Exp. Date _____

Signature _____ Day Phone _____
__ Bill Me (U.S. institutional orders only. Purchase order required.)

Purchase order # _____
                 Federal Tax ID13559302   **GST 89102 8052**

Name _____

Address _____

_____

Phone _____ E-mail _____

For more information about Jossey-Bass, visit our Web site at www.josseybass.com

TL97   **Building Faculty Learning Communities**
        Milton D. Cox, Laurie Richlin
        A very effective way to address institutional challenges is a faculty learning
        community. FLCs are useful for preparing future faculty, reinvigorating
        senior faculty, and implementing new courses, curricula, or campus
        initiatives. The results of FLCs parallel those of student learning
        communities, such as retention, deeper learning, respect for others, and
        greater civic participation. This volume describe FLCs from a practitioner's
        perspective, with plenty of advice, wisdom, and lessons for starting your
        own FLC.
        ISBN: 0-7879-7568-0

TL96   **Online Student Ratings of Instruction**
        Trav D. Johnson, D. Lynn Sorenson
        Many institutions are adopting Web-based student ratings of instruction, or
        are considering doing it, because online systems have the potential to save
        time and money among other benefits. But they also present a number of
        challenges. The authors of this volume have firsthand experience with
        electronic ratings of instruction. They identify the advantages, consider costs
        and benefits, explain their solutions, and provide recommendations on how
        to facilitate online ratings.
        ISBN: 0-7879-7262-2

TL95   **Problem-Based Learning in the Information Age**
        Dave S. Knowlton, David C. Sharp
        Provides information about theories and practices associated with problem-
        based learning, a pedagogy that allows students to become more engaged in
        their own education by actively interpreting information. Today's professors
        are adopting problem-based learning across all disciplines to facilitate a
        broader, modern definition of what it means to learn. Authors provide
        practical experience about designing useful problems, creating conducive
        learning environments, facilitating students' activities, and assessing
        students' efforts at problem solving.
        ISBN: 0-7879-7172-3

TL94   **Technology: Taking the Distance out of Learning**
        Margit Misangyi Watts
        This volume addresses the possibilities and challenges of computer
        technology in higher education. The contributors examine the pressures to
        use technology, the reasons not to, the benefits of it, the feeling of being a
        learner as well as a teacher, the role of distance education, and the place of
        computers in the modern world. Rather than discussing only specific
        successes or failures, this issue addresses computers as a new cultural
        symbol and begins meaningful conversations about technology in general
        and how it affects education in particular.
        ISBN: 0-7879-6989-3

TL93   **Valuing and Supporting Undergraduate Research**
        Joyce Kinkead
        The authors gathered in this volume share a deep belief in the value of
        undergraduate research. Research helps students develop skills in problem
        solving, critical thinking, and communication, and undergraduate
        researchers' work can contribute to an institution's quest to further

knowledge and help meet societal challenges. Chapters provide an overview of undergraduate research, explore programs at different types of institutions, and offer suggestions on how faculty members can find ways to work with undergraduate researchers.
ISBN: 0-7879-6907-9

TL92   **The Importance of Physical Space in Creating Supportive Learning Environments**
Nancy Van Note Chism, Deborah J. Bickford
The lack of extensive dialogue on the importance of learning spaces in higher education environments prompted the essays in this volume. Chapter authors look at the topic of learning spaces from a variety of perspectives, elaborating on the relationship between physical space and learning, arguing for an expanded notion of the concept of learning spaces and furnishings, talking about the context within which decision making for learning spaces takes place, and discussing promising approaches to the renovation of old learning spaces and the construction of new ones.
ISBN: 0-7879-6344-5

TL91   **Assessment Strategies for the On-Line Class: From Theory to Practice**
Rebecca S. Anderson, John F. Bauer, Bruce W. Speck
Addresses the kinds of questions that instructors need to ask themselves as they begin to move at least part of their students' work to an on-line format. Presents an initial overview of the need for evaluating students' on-line work with the same care that instructors give to the work in hard-copy format. Helps guide instructors who are considering using on-line learning in conjunction with their regular classes, as well as those interested in going totally on-line.
ISBN: 0-7879-6343-7

TL90   **Scholarship in the Postmodern Era: New Venues, New Values, New Visions**
Kenneth J. Zahorski
A little over a decade ago, Ernest Boyer's *Scholarship Reconsidered* burst upon the academic scene, igniting a robust national conversation that maintains its vitality to this day. This volume aims at advancing that important conversation. Its first section focuses on the new settings and circumstances in which the act of scholarship is being played out; its second identifies and explores the fresh set of values currently informing today's scholarly practices; and its third looks to the future of scholarship, identifying trends, causative factors, and potentialities that promise to shape scholars and their scholarship in the new millennium.
ISBN: 0-7879-6293-7

TL89   **Applying the Science of Learning to University Teaching and Beyond**
Diane F. Halpern, Milton D. Hakel
Seeks to build on empirically validated learning activities to enhance what and how much is learned and how well and how long it is remembered. Demonstrates that the movement for a real science of learning—the application of scientific principles to the study of learning—has taken hold both under the controlled conditions of the laboratory and in the messy real-world settings where most of us go about the business of teaching and learning.
ISBN: 0-7879-5791-7

TL88   **Fresh Approaches to the Evaluation of Teaching**
        Christopher Knapper, Patricia Cranton
        Describes a number of alternative approaches, including interpretive and
        critical evaluation, use of teaching portfolios and teaching awards,
        performance indicators and learning outcomes, technology-mediated
        evaluation systems, and the role of teacher accreditation and teaching
        scholarship in instructional evaluation.
        ISBN: 0-7879-5789-5

TL87   **Techniques and Strategies for Interpreting Student Evaluations**
        Karron G. Lewis
        Focuses on all phases of the student rating process—from data-gathering
        methods to presentation of results. Topics include methods of encouraging
        meaningful evaluations, mid-semester feedback, uses of quality teams and
        focus groups, and creating questions that target individual faculty needs and
        interest.
        ISBN: 0-7879-5789-5

TL86   **Scholarship Revisited: Perspectives on the Scholarship of Teaching**
        Carolin Kreber
        Presents the outcomes of a Delphi Study conducted by an international
        panel of academics working in faculty evaluation scholarship and
        postsecondary teaching and learning. Identifies the important components of
        scholarship of teaching, defines its characteristics and outcomes, and
        explores its most pressing issues.
        ISBN: 0-7879-5447-0

TL85   **Beyond Teaching to Mentoring**
        Alice G. Reinarz, Eric R. White
        Offers guidelines to optimizing student learning through classroom activities
        as well as peer, faculty, and professional mentoring. Addresses mentoring
        techniques in technical training, undergraduate business, science, and liberal
        arts studies, health professions, international study, and interdisciplinary
        work.
        ISBN: 0-7879-5617-1

TL84   **Principles of Effective Teaching in the Online Classroom**
        Renée E. Weiss, Dave S. Knowlton, Bruce W. Speck
        Discusses structuring the online course, utilizing resources from the World
        Wide Web and using other electronic tools and technology to enhance
        classroom efficiency. Addresses challenges unique to the online classroom
        community, including successful communication strategies, performance
        evaluation, academic integrity, and accessibility for disabled students.
        ISBN: 0-7879-5615-5

TL83   **Evaluating Teaching in Higher Education: A Vision for the Future**
        Katherine E. Ryan
        Analyzes the strengths and weaknesses of current approaches to evaluating
        teaching and recommends practical strategies for improving current
        evaluation methods and developing new ones. Provides an overview of new
        techniques such as peer evaluations, portfolios, and student ratings of
        instructors and technologies.
        ISBN: 0-7879-5448-9

NEW DIRECTIONS FOR TEACHING AND LEARNING IS NOW AVAILABLE ONLINE AT WILEY INTERSCIENCE

What is Wiley InterScience?

Wiley InterScience is the dynamic online content service from John Wiley & Sons delivering the full text of over 300 leading scientific, technical, medical, and professional journals, plus major reference works, the acclaimed Current Protocols laboratory manuals, and even the full text of select Wiley print books online.

What are some special features of Wiley InterScience?

Wiley Interscience Alerts is a service that delivers table of contents via e-mail for any journal available on Wiley InterScience as soon as a new issue is published online.
EarlyView is Wiley's exclusive service presenting individual articles online as soon as they are ready, even before the release of the compiled print issue. These articles are complete, peer-reviewed, and citable.
CrossRef is the innovative multi-publisher reference linking system enabling readers to move seamlessly from a reference in a journal article to the cited publication, typically located on a different server and published by a different publisher.

How can I access Wiley InterScience?

Visit http://www.interscience.wiley.com.

Guest Users can browse Wiley InterScience for unrestricted access to journal tables of contents and article abstracts, or use the powerful search engine.
Registered Users are provided with a *Personal Home Page* to store and manage customized alerts, searches, and links to favorite journals and articles. Additionally, Registered Users can view free online sample issues and preview selected material from major reference works.
Licensed Customers are entitled to access full-text journal articles in PDF, with select journals also offering full-text HTML.

How do I become an Authorized User?

Authorized Users are individuals authorized by a paying Customer to have access to the journals in Wiley InterScience. For example, a university that subscribes to Wiley journals is considered to be the Customer.
Faculty, staff and students authorized by the university to have access to those journals in Wiley InterScience are Authorized Users. Users should contact their library for information on which Wiley journals they have access to in Wiley InterScience.